Every Child's Right

Every Child's Right

ACADEMIC TALENT DEVELOPMENT BY CHOICE, NOT CHANCE

Lauren A. Sosniak and Nina Hersch Gabelko

Teachers College, Columbia University
New York and London

To Frankie Temple
Assistant Dean, University of California–Berkeley,
Graduate School of Education
The Academic Talent Development Program would not have started,
and could not have persisted, without her.

———————————————

Published by Teachers College Press, 1234 Amsterdam Avenue, New York, NY 10027

Library of Congress Cataloging-in-Publication Data

Sosniak, Lauren A.
   Every child's right : academic talent development by choice, not chance / Lauren A. Sosniak and Nina Hersch Gabelko.
      p.   cm.
   Includes bibliographical references and index.
   ISBN 978-0-8077-4870-1 (pbk : alk. paper) — ISBN 978-0-8077-4871-8 (cloth : alk. paper)
   1. Gifted children—Education.   2. Gifted children—Identification.   3. Academic achievement.   I. Gabelko, Nina Hersch, 1942–   II. Title.

   LC3993.S59 2008
   371.95—dc22

                                                                          2007045115

ISBN: 978-0-8077-4870-1 (paper)
ISBN: 978-0-8077-4871-8 (cloth)

Printed on acid-free paper
Manufactured in the United States of America

15   14   13   12   11   10   09   08   8   7   6   5   4   3   2   1

Contents

 # Preface

Lauren, an Appreciation

AT THE ACADEMIC TALENT DEVELOPMENT PROGRAM (ATDP) Lauren A. Sosniak was known as the "Maven." She was so named by Lloyd Nebres because she really was one. She had started her academic career working with Benjamin Bloom on the landmark Development of Talent study, and she carried forward the passion she developed for studying ways to develop talent in all children and youth. Of course, in her work with ATDP, she was ever the ideal researcher and academician. The ethical stands she took and the careful attention she paid to every detail assured that her research was always to a standard that outstripped by a mile the demands of any institutional review board and was warmly received by a wide community of readers.

Lauren wore the ATDP maven crown. Actually, it's an old paper Burger King crown that says Latin Verbs on one side and Maven on the other—waste not, want not. And actually she didn't wear it voluntarily; we would put it on her head when we sought her council. She didn't like it much, but the rest of us thought it terribly funny and we tried to make her hold court. She refused, and instead took people out to lunch for deep conversations. That did look like she was holding court, but always a democratic one.

Offhand, I can't think of an area in which she had not read widely and to which she could not add interesting insights. We'd listen in awe as she switched topics when she chatted with different people, moving effortlessly from the stock market, to the accomplishments of Lance Armstrong, to any facet of politics. She loved music—classical, popular, and liturgical.

Folks who otherwise try hard to avoid meetings would always check first to see if Lauren would be present, before they'd decide to cut. If she was there, so were they. Over the years, her contributions to ATDP faculty meetings—even the ones where she intended to be a fly-on-the-wall notetaker—created opportunities for teachers to become aware that the things they were doing were both extraordinary and acknowledged by people they respected. Lauren could put seemingly unrelated or even incompatible points of view and ideas together in unique ways that encouraged participants to work together to further develop their own academic talents.

Creation of choices—like the ones we write about in this book, especially ones that children and youth might make for themselves and still be assured that their choices would be supported by the community—was the cornerstone of her work and her life. She actually dedicated herself to doing those things that most of us list as things needing to be done. Lauren was a loyal and loving friend, yet she always seemed so surprised when others told her how much they loved and admired her.

Lauren died at the start of January 2006. The goal of completing this book was paramount to her and she never stopped working on it. The prospect of completing the book without her was not a happy one, but a promise is a promise. However, it never became a solo effort. Gary Griffin, who had hired her for her first professorship way back in the 1980s and who was her dear friend and mentor, worked with me every step of the way. His wisdom and knowledge were always offered with a light (but firm) hand and were frequently delivered couched in great humor, though any foolishness was subjected to a bright light. For example, just as Lauren was the Maven, Gary named me the "Comma Queen," a dubious honor, richly deserved.

All that you'll enjoy in this book is directly attributable to Lauren, and if not directly to Lauren then to Gary. Any errors you find are mine—as are the commas.

—N.H.G.

Acknowledgments

THROUGHOUT THE WHOLE PROCESS of writing this book, Lauren and I received the unwavering support, encouragement, and tolerance of our "outside of ATDP" families: Anatoly, David, and Katrina Gabelko; Gary Griffin; Frankie Temple; Randy Sosniak; Marilyn Chambliss; Roy, Pam, Jordan, Brandon, and Austin Meyers; and Lauren's colleagues Philip Jackson, Mary Driscoll, Susan Stodolsky, Mark Smylie, Corinna (Bunty) Ethington, John Smart, Margaret Harrington, Lee Schulman, and Kathryn Sloan.

ATDP tenacity awards go to: Flossie Lewis, for over 25 years, instructor and resident *tzedic* (a very righteous, wise, just person); Frank C. Worrell, nearing 20 years, combined, as ATDP faculty director, professor and director of the University of California (UC)–Berkeley's school psychology program, and ATDP instructor, head counselor, and researcher; Nancy A. Mellor, 20 years of collaboration with ATDP, CHA House program founder, middle school mathematics teachers, and now, superintendent extraordinaire; Beverly Vandiver, a decade as ATDP visiting professor, instructor, head program counselor, researcher—all the while a Penn State professor; Lloyd R. Nebres, who started as a student worker over 20 years ago, then became an instructor, computer maven, mentor extraordinaire, philosopher, photographer, web master, graphic artist, and contributor to this book; Carrie S. Brown, whose encyclopedic knowledge, infinite patience, insistence that she read everything for manners and tone before the director sent it out, and grace under pressure has kept every phase of ATDP moving in the right direction for 20 years; Cristina Flores, who grew from a 12-year-old ATDP student to outreach program creator and staff member; Casey D. Cheung, who also began as an ATDP student and grew into an astounding logician who can work with scads of variables in mind and think years ahead; and Edan Dekel, who in less than 10 years developed and taught 25 ATDP classes. We also recognize Laura Shefler, instructor, staffer, and Magic Carpet Reading Club program developer; Alexis Dekel, champion of mathematics and dance (combined); Gary Hsueh; Abigail Lustig; Candace Nolan-Grant; Susan Bennett; Yoshiko Tagami; Adena Young; Norman I. Lustig; and Laurie Mireles—all have made important contributions to ATDP.

Each ATDP instructor has contributed to our story. We list by name those whose nonstop contributions exceed a decade: George Austin, Heidi Boley, Lyda Butler, Doris Castillo-Shadic, Jack Coakley, M. P. Echeverriarza Espinola, Robert Fabini, Anatoly Gabelko, Gary Graves, Philippe Henri, Mary Sue Kennedy, Steve Kirby, Gary Kitajo, Enrique Lessa, Flossie Lewis, Cheryl Lilhanand, Elise Lustig, Heather MacLeod, Julie MacNamara, Grant Mellor, Mike Meneghetti, Carol Ponzio, Laura Schooley, Arijit Sen, Catherine Terry, and Gemma Whelan.

ATDP has been cheered on and supported by university professors and administrators. We thank in particular Genaro Padilla, Anita Madrid, Daniel Perlstein, Joe Castro, Angelica Stacey, Rhona Weinstein, Susan Jenkins, Clark McKown, Paul Ammon, Della Peretti, and Dan Zimmerlin. We have very special thanks for the kind souls in departments across the campus who graciously shared their classrooms, permitting young students to "try on" university life. We want to heap praise on the staff and administration of the UC Berkeley Early Academic Outreach Program (EAOP) for their passion for collaboration with ATDP. We thank the entire UC Berkeley Graduate School of Education, especially those who enjoy middle schoolers' singing and laughing in their corridors.

We thank public school administrators who have given of their wisdom and support: Dr. Kaye E. Burnside, Dr. Debbie Ann LaSalle, Dr. Rhitu Kannah, Ms. Jan Link, Dr. Hoover Liddell, Ms. Helene Gordon, Ms. Bettye Saunders, Ms. Ann Kirton, and Ms. Rory Bled. Particular praise goes to the many classroom teachers who have become ATDP's best recruiters of underserved students. We thank ATDP students, present and past, for each one has contributed to our story and taught us a lesson worth knowing.

 **Introduction**

OUR GOAL IN THIS BOOK is to influence the national conversation about developing academic talent. This is not a romantic book: It is not an account of all our children developing academic talent. Rather, it is a book about children and youth developing academic talent in a context that is inclusive and welcoming. We hope that the story we have to tell, which is a blend of theory and very concrete and long-standing instances of educational practice, will provide compelling visions of greater and more broadly distributed possibilities for the academic education of American youth.

Ours is a story of possibility—the possibility for significant academic achievement and intellectual engagement of American children and youth, across race, ethnicity, and social class, with students learning together, sharing interests and aspirations, and accomplishing more than might seem possible.

The book is part existence proof and part exhortation. It aims to provoke thought and action. It speaks to education both in and outside of school. Because we want to influence a national conversation about educational possibilities, we hope that the wide range of stakeholders in education will consider the possibilities we present. Each group of stakeholders needs to be included in our conversation, each of them needs to be represented at the discussion table—undergraduate and graduate students, novice and experienced educators and researchers, policymakers, families, teachers, school district administrators, community and school board members.

THE ACADEMIC TALENT DEVELOPMENT PROGRAM

The Academic Talent Development Program (ATDP) doesn't try to do it all. But its staff have learned how to do something differently and, we think, better. That "something" is the development of academic talent. We describe the program in this book from its beginnings as a fairly standard gifted students program through its evolution into something with much richer learning experiences that serves a more diverse and larger community of students. Throughout the book we follow journeys: ATDP's journey, the journeys of individuals and groups, the journeys of whole communities.

When the earliest version of today's program began in 1981, the first director chose to affiliate with the Johns Hopkins Academic Talent Search Program (created and run for many years by the late Julian Stanley). The UC Berkeley Gifted Program, as it was called then, was a West Coast outpost for the Johns Hopkins vision. It seemed a sensible decision at the time. Johns Hopkins University and UC Berkeley had (and have) a great deal in common as academic institutions, and it was not yet quite so obvious that early identification—talent *searches*—were likely to have so little long-term payoff for the Berkeley program.

The searches seemed out of touch with the needs and interests of youth and parents in the Bay Area. And the approach seemed out of touch with the growing body of research on the development of talent. After careful study, after thinking through what might be offered and how the program could defend different offerings, the program moved slowly from a focus on *searching for giftedness* to a focus on *developing talent*.

We will travel with the Academic Talent Development Program staff and directors as they made deliberate and purposeful decisions about how this program would wend its way through the minefields of the language and ideas of talent. The program directors have had to decide where the program stands with respect to long-standing conflicts and controversies. The decisions they have made for the program have had consequences. The program recruits and admits some children and youth and not others; it offers some educational opportunities and not others.

ATDP is different. It begins with the premise that the work of the program is to create talent, build it, grow it, develop it—certainly not to seek to mine or unearth it. Following from this, ATDP defines for its constituency the specific talents it is designed to promote, and creates conditions that, it hopes, will support children and youth who are interested in one of these areas and willing to work hard. It is not concerned about whether the students qualify as talented based on their test scores. It is concerned with providing a program that best enhances the curiosity of children and youth and helps them develop their academic talents.

Thus we must address two questions: Who does come? and How does the director know that all the program deliberations about whom to serve have had any consequence? We start by looking at how ATDP students stack up in relation to the traditional gifted and talented concerns about scores on norm-referenced standardized tests of aptitude or achievement.

To examine whether the student population has become more inclusive in terms of position on a norm-referenced standardized test scale as program changes were put into place, we compare 2 years here: 1990, the first year of the revised ATDP history, and 1996, a year that reflects changes made since 1990. In Chapter 1 we revisit these two years and add data for 2002, the year that ATDP reach its enrollment capacity.

In the summer of 1990, ATDP was still in the process of moving away from searching for gifted students and toward the growing of academic talent. That year about 80% of its students would have qualified with ease for most gifted programs anywhere in the country. As relationships were formed with individual schools and districts, with families and their friends, and as multiple indicators were considered, the student population became more diverse.

By the summer of 1996, the program more fully aimed at developing academic talent. That year, 25% of the ATDP students scored at or above the 97th percentile on the verbal and 36% scored at or above the 97th percentile on the math portion of a standardized achievement test. But 41% of the ATDP student population had scores lower than the traditional cut-score expectations for most gifted and talented programs. Additionally, 13% of the ATDP students in 1996 reported no scores; the absence of a standardized test score likely would have excluded these students from most traditional gifted and talented programs. To put it another way, by 1996, about half of the students ATDP served would not have merited attention from most of the gifted and talented programs in the country by virtue of their scores on standardized tests of verbal and mathematical abilities.

ATDP students are diverse not only with respect to test scores but also in many ways that traditional gifted and talented programs seem to struggle with. For example, in the summer of 1993 nearly 27% of the students served by the program came from homes with annual family incomes at or below the national poverty line. Father's education for that population included about 27% who had not earned a 4-year college degree. For mothers, the percentage was 36%.

These students attended class successfully alongside students whose parents had completed graduate degrees. We will show that it is possible to serve such a population well, even with such diversity in test scores, family background, and economic status.

OVERVIEW OF THE BOOK

Since it's a national conversation that we seek to impact and change, this book is intended to be conversational and friendly. We want you to enjoy the book, and since we're both storytellers, we hope that you'll also laugh at our jokes when they appear.

As a discussion of inequities is inherent in, if not the cornerstone of, our conversation, we are direct in our presentation and also direct in disclosing what is required of society and its schools in order for academic talent development to become a matter of choice, and no longer remain a matter of chance—something to be grown, not mined. We hope that our directness will assist others in moving their own communities away from mining for academic talent and will support them in their joyous work of growing it.

A word about the organization of the book might be useful to you. Chapters 1 and 4 set out the framework, theoretical and practical. The two chapters that follow each of them provide the all-important context within which our stories evolve and our evidence is presented.

In Chapter 1, "Grow Talent; Don't Mine It," we summarize the world of giftedness and talent and present the view that researchers and educators have historically treated both as if they were gems to be mined. Our discussion develops the idea of shifting the collective image of talent from being an innate characteristic to an alterable variable. We show that talent is not a strictly limited commodity, but rather it becomes plentiful when cultivated in any of a range of fertile fields. We introduce the Academic Talent Development Program and present it throughout the book as an example of a long-standing, self-supporting summer program that shifted from mining to growing talent, and show the program as it welcomes a wide range of youth into a community of scholarship.

In Chapter 2, "Welcome to the Academic Conversation!" we present ATDP as a welcoming community, in which the academic advantages or disadvantages one may have had before arriving at the program are merely facts of our larger social life which may influence the support the program provides but not the aims the program holds. ATDP staff truly believe that their program can help to develop academic talent in all who take the idea and the program seriously. In order to experience the community as we present it, we encourage readers to try on the roles of program students and instructors to experience the depth of the academic conversation, to participate in the student-to-student, student-to-instructor, and student-to-academic discipline relationships as they develop among groups of students who, except for the program, are unlikely to have ever met. During this time, students learn firsthand what it is about specific disciplines that is exciting enough to cause people to dedicate their careers to their study. Over time, ATDP students also learn how to navigate and negotiate among and between choices, continually widen and reevaluate their own goals, and refine their own academic plans.

Chapter 3, "When Learning Is Child's Play," takes us into the world of possibilities available to children in the years before they are old enough to attend middle school (Grades K–6). As with Chapter 2, we show a wide range of learners from a wider range of backgrounds developing fast friendships and firm understandings of who "we" are. Susan Engle's (2005) outstanding description of children as learners captures the goals and context of the ATDP Elementary Division's vision of children as:

> budding experts who absorb information and ideas from experts within their culture, and who practice, amassing strategies, information, and techniques that lift their thinking to a higher level within that domain or discipline. Their knowledge therefore is both culturally specific and domain specific. Children's skills emerge from experience with a certain set of materials and goals and reflect the community and habits within which they are learned and used. (p. 171)

So, as you prepare to experience Elementary Division, prepare to imagine, play, and try on a huge range of roles, from the first-grade magic mantle of a mythological character to the infinite universe of a fourth-grade theoretical physicist.

In Chapter 4, "Every Child's Right: Academic Talent Development in All Communities and Classrooms," we begin from the understanding that in order to be well educated, all of our children must be educated together. We also show how far our social institutions are from applying that understanding in practice. We hope to convince you that if we keep our goal of "growing academic talent" unwaveringly before us, and if we are candid in acknowledging not only the barriers students face but also the conditions requisite for success, we can attain our goal. The chapter is a complex one, as it brings together ideas from a number of disciplines, including political science, psychology, sociology, philosophy, and more. But we don't think that it is complicated, at least not if you keep in mind that we are trying to create a more unified way of offering possibilities to all children and youth. We ask you to examine barriers—some commonly perceived ones and some we worry still remain invisible—to educating "all of our children together." Then we ask you to consider the social and educational conditions that support educational achievement.

We have divided the chapter into three parts: First, we present an overview of education as it presently appears inside and outside of school, including some historic barriers to academic talent development. We then deconstruct some ideas and conditions that create or exacerbate problems presently preventing academic talent development for many children and youth. Finally, we identify beliefs and conditions required for offering an ATDP-type of education to all children, in all classrooms. Aside from the ATDP-specific examples that put information into the context of first-person experiences, most of the other data we offer are available elsewhere, but we present these data and these stories here because we ask you to consider a more unified view of talent and its development—a view that is twined and three-dimensional, a view of the interrelationships, misconceptions, dichotomies, and rich possibilities we need to work with if we are to provide the inclusive learning communities we seek to form.

Chapter 5, "Changing College-Going from Chance to Choice," was inspired by a statement made many years ago by a student that showed how invisible college remains to many American young people. He said to his mentor, "Oh, we always knew we were going to college. We just didn't know what college was." In this chapter we explore not only what college is at the end of the first decade of the twenty-first century, but also how one might get there from here. We present practices, within the context of ATDP and its partners, that have been successful for a number of years. And we present, from the students' view and in students' voices, ways in which successful practices can be offered to much larger groups of students than are presently aware, informed, prepared, and competitive for a successful college career.

In Chapter 6, "The Gift of Community and the Community of Gifts," we offer stories and descriptive statistics to show how being an integral part of an academic community—one designed to grow talent—does, and does not, change lives. We offer both the personal experience and the descriptions in an attempt to demonstrate that communities of practice and academically rich neighborhoods, which have the potential to add so much to the competence and passion children, youth, and adults might bring to their life activities, aren't bounded by where a person lives physically. We show them to be places where people choose to be and are invited to join; as places where some choose to remain as part of the community by taking it with them wherever they go. We present huge contrasts in the ways sending schools represent themselves and their students in order to show how ambitious communities of practice support how students define and redefine themselves as they guide students from novice to expert. We provide as an exemplar the experiences of groups of students of color from low-performing rural and urban schools who have attended ATDP over a period of 20 years, including institutional and circumstantial roadblocks and detours the students and ATDP have faced along the way. We also remind readers that the schools cannot do it all, and exhort all who are dedicated to making academic talent development a viable choice for all of our children—together—to create their own version of ATDP experiences. We urge serious consideration of the possibilities of utilizing time outside of school, especially the summer, for permitting students to see how rich and exciting discipline-specific learning is, and how much more they can learn than they would ever have imagined, and what close relationships they can forge with others whom they might otherwise never have met, in places they had not known existed.

All student and teacher names have been changed throughout the book, to respect the privilege of sharing the information they have provided. With their permission and with great admiration, ATDP staff, instructor Flossie Lewis, a few university faculty, and district-level administrators are referred to by their actual names.

Grow Talent, Don't Mine It

IN THIS CHAPTER WE DESCRIBE the confusing world of *talent*, of *genius*, of *giftedness*, and the variety of other terms associated with human performance at its best. We describe the decisions the Academic Talent Development Program has made, and the rationale for those decisions, for what counts as talent and what does not, and who counts as talented and who does not. And we offer what we hope you will find to be compelling evidence that the ATDP directors have made the right choices.

WHAT'S TALENT? WHO'S TALENTED?

Casual conversation about *talent* tends to overlook or even be indifferent to most, but probably not all, of the tensions, complexities, and controversies associated professionally with the word. In everyday conversation we comfortably label as *talented* any number of people with a wide range of knowledge and skill. For example, surely most of us would agree that the cellist Yo-Yo Ma deserves the label. And many of us might similarly label as talented the teenager who quickly brings order to the mess we have made trying to network wirelessly a set of household computers, printers, and other equipment.

Then there is Chad Fernandez who appeared on the NBC *Today Show* in the summer of 2003, supervised by a *Guinness World Records* researcher, to take aim at the record for the longest skateboard rail grind. (As the *Today Show*'s Web site explained at the time, a skateboard *rail grind* involves "lifting the skateboard at speed off the ground, sliding—or 'grinding'—along a metal bar or rail, and landing back on all four wheels.") The old record was 21.32 feet; Chad set a new record of 36.75 feet. Is Chad talented? It depends, doesn't it, on how much you know about and value skateboarding?

A quick look through any edition of the *Guinness World Records* raises many questions about talent. One edition of that record book notes that Billie Jean King (USA) won more Wimbledon titles than any other woman. Both authors of this book would call Billie Jean King talented. We are absolutely certain about that. But what about Marianne Gille, from Sweden, who in 2003 held the record for keeping a grape suspended in the air above her mouth for 4.81 seconds? Before you dismiss Ms. Gille too quickly, you might want to try this at home. More important, you might ask yourself if the talent associated with keeping a grape suspended in the air above one's mouth is really that different from, say, skill at hurling a discus or a javelin or a shot put to a new Olympic record, or holding a high note at an important moment in an opera?

Any answer to the question of who is talented and who is not turns out to tell as much about our values as it tells about the person we are labeling. Talent is both content and context dependent. One is talented at some thing or in some way. And whether one's knowledge and skill is recognized as talent depends on how much that knowledge or skill matters to others (cf. Csikszentmihalyi & Robinson, 1986).

Tannenbaum (1958) put it this way:

> Man is capable of mastering an almost endless variety of skills, but it remains for society to judge which shall be regarded as high-level talent. Such judgments are rooted in history and can be fully understood only in light of the fact that society's estimate and encouragement of high achievement change with the spirit of the age. (p. 22)

Getzels and Dillon (1973), writing similarly, offer these examples:

> In wartime, the society tends to exalt and reward talents for killing and destroying and will legitimize allied talents otherwise thought criminal. In more pedestrian pursuits, the society will reward a talent for wheeling-and-dealing in a business executive or entrepreneur but will punish it in an accountant or bank examiner; it will value creative display in its advertising but not in its surgery. (p. 704)

More recently, Melanie Thernstrom (2005) offered these examples: "Matchmaking requires a peculiar, innate talent, as rare a gift as being able to shoot a basketball through a hoop again and again. No one does it flawlessly, but some people are much better than others" (p. 37).

We offer Ms. Thernstrom's example at this point because it helps us move from casual conversation about talent that is mostly indifferent to subtleties of the word to professional conversation that, often but not always, takes its language much more seriously. Note that Ms. Thernstrom used the word *talent* in the same sentence and with the same intended meaning as the word *gift*. And in both cases she added qualifiers: *innate* talent; *rare* gift. Ms. Thernstrom is leading us toward the potential complexities and controversies associated with the word and the world of talent.

IS SHE GIFTED? IS HE TALENTED?
WHO STUDIES IT? WHO CARES?

The academic community does not take the idea and example of talent as casually as most of us do in everyday conversation, at least not much of the time. The scholarly world needs definitions and distinctions and qualities that can be measured. As researchers have wound their way around the study of human performance at its best, words have been added and subtracted, and over time there has been a gradual shift in the dominant language.

The family of words associated with human performance at its best includes *genius, giftedness, talent, expertise, exceptional accomplishment, human extraordinariness, prodigious performance, superior human ability,* and so on. The most prominent, of course, are *giftedness* and *talent. Genius* came earliest (the late 1800s and early 1900s) and rapidly fell out of favor; *expertise,* a noted part of the cognitive science literature since at least 1985, has not yet made a serious foothold in scholarly work involving children and youth.

Harold Rugg (1924) early on captured the relative orientation of the various words:

> The number of children of conspicuous ability in our schools is probably large. Whether it is one million or ten thousand will depend on one's definition of "giftedness." Certainly, the "gifted" themselves are graduated in ability down from levels of true genius—shall we say one in a million—to those of conspicuous ability or talent—shall we say one or even more in a hundred? (p. 93)

IT'S LESS ABOUT DIFFERENCES IN KIND,
MORE ABOUT SPEED OR AMOUNT

As *giftedness* and *talent* became the two predominant words describing human performance at its best, various scholars struggled to explain distinctions between the two words. Gagné (2003) captures one well-accepted distinction, writing that giftedness and talent "roughly correspond to the ideas of potential/aptitude and achievement or, in other words, to the distinction between natural abilities and systematically developed skills" (p. 60). Gottfredson (2003) captures another well-accepted distinction, which allows both words to represent potential. Her explanation involves hierarchical considerations: "*giftedness* represents fairly broad abilities and *talent* more specific ones" (italics in original, p. 26). The broad abilities typically refer back to something labeled *general intelligence* or *academic aptitude.* The more specific abilities typically refer back to a changing range of talents including, at various times, artistic, dramatic, mechanical, scientific, musical, and leadership talent. The first federal legislation related to education for "the gifted and talented" included "psychomotor ability" also (see below), but interestingly, that form of talent was dropped in subsequent legislative action and does not seem to have found a place in any gifted and talented definition or program.

The two distinctions—broad versus specific, and potential versus accomplishment—appear widely accepted and long enduring. They also are frequently commingled, including in legal code. The *Delaware State Code* from 1953, for example, offered these definitions:

> "Gifted children" means children between the chronological ages of four and twenty-one who are endowed by nature with high intellectual capacity and who have a native capacity for high potential intellectual attainment and scholastic achievement.
>
> "Talented children" means children between the chronological ages of four and twenty-one who have demonstrated superior talents, aptitudes, or abilities, outstanding leadership qualities and abilities, or consistently remarkable performance in the mechanics, manipulative skills, the art of expression of ideas, oral or written, music, art, human relations or any other worthwhile line of human achievement. (Article 14, Section 3162, as reported in Zettel, 1979, p. 63)

Almost 20 years later, in 1971, the U.S. Commissioner of Education, Sidney Marland Jr., proposed an essentially similar definition—including both distinctions, commingled—that subsequently was written into federal legislation:

> Gifted and talented children are those identified by professionally qualified persons, who by virtue of outstanding abilities are capable of high performance. . . .
>
> Children capable of high performance include those with demonstrated achievement and/or potential ability in any of the following areas, singly or in combination: (1) general intellectual ability, (2) specific academic aptitude, (3) creative or productive thinking, (4) leadership ability, (5) visual and performing arts, (6) psychomotor ability (*Public Law 91-230, section 806*, as reported in U.S. Department of Education, 1993, p. 16).

Notwithstanding all the efforts to make distinctions between the terms, in practice *gifted and talented* has become a singular phrase in the education and legislative communities.

What's Potential All About? To Whom Is It Important?

Why is there so much interest in the potential of children and youth, whether broad or narrow? The answer is almost always offered passionately. In 1924 Rugg wrote:

I believe that both from the standpoint of the development of each individual to the highest possible point and from the standpoint of the greatest contribution to the improvement of society, the gifted in each town and city in our country should be discovered, organized into working groups, and given the most far-reaching course of training our intelligence can organize. (p. 110)

In other words, Rugg believed, like many before him (remember Plato) and many still today, that there are groups of children and youth who, by virtue of some special quality or qualities, need and deserve special educational provisions that will support their eventual leadership in society. In 1958 the argument was presented this way:

It is important to give gifted children the education they need because society needs them badly. Our economy needs them, and we must have them for national security. They are our most valuable human resource because they maintain our culture and create the advances in all fields. Future generations depend on them. (Havighurst, Hersey, Meister, Corning, & Terman, 1958, p. 13)

Getzels and Dillon (1973) wrote of a prevailing point of view that "children with exceptional talents are often seen as sources of Manpower to be trained and directed, if not conscripted, into the service of technological progress and economic advancement" (pp. 703–704). From Horowitz and O'Brien (1985) we hear: "The gifted and the talented among our children represent one of the richest of our human resource potentials. We lose every time the educational experiences of these children do not maximize their functional capabilities" (p. 453). And, more recently, Kirk, Gallagher, and Anastasiow (2000) write:

Society has a special interest in children who are gifted, both as individuals and as potential contributors to society's well-being. As individuals, they have the same right to full development as do all children. In addition, many of the leaders, scientists, and poets of the next generation will come from the current group of children who are gifted and talented. Few societies can afford to ignore that potential. (p. 116)

Who belongs in the group of children and youth who need and deserve a special education? That depends. Almost always, inclusion or exclusion relies on comparison: We are looking for children and youth who are better than others the same age tested on the same measure. The gifted or talented fall at the upper margin of some norm distribution. We are looking for what is rare, extreme, nonnormal, or exceptional. We are looking for the children and youth who are faster than others at picking up a body of knowledge or set of skills. We are looking for the children and youth who, at some moment, quite visibly know or can do more than others their same age. Our methods of identifying gifted and talented youth typically have less to do with any special qualities (differences in kind) and more to do with differences in speed or amount.

All the Gifted Kids There's Room For: Yours, Mine, Ours, or None

How exceptional does a child need to be to be included in the category of gifted or talented? Again, it depends. Gagné (2003) asserts that "any individuals whose outstanding skill mastery places them among the top 10 percent within their occupational field should be recognized as talented" (p. 62). Some scholars are stricter in what they advocate, and others are more lenient. In the opening chapter of the 1958 National Society for the Study of Education (NSSE) volume, *Education for the Gifted*, Havighurst and colleagues posed the challenge of the volume this way:

> We devote this yearbook, not to the 2 or 5 per cent with the highest intelligence quotients [as had been the standard since the work of Terman], but to the 20 per cent with promise of exceptionally good performance in a variety of areas of constructive activity. (p. 19)

This norm-referenced approach to identifying the gifted or talented allows for identifying as many or as few youth as there might be resources to support. Or as many or as few as there is political will to argue for. It also allows for many debates about who is included and who is not: debates between parents and school administrators about the percentage or two in a child's test score or a school's standards that would include a son or daughter in some special education program; debates between teachers and administrators about the best range of abilities for optimal instruction; debates among professors about what the words *gifted* and *talented* truly mean.

And yes, parents are very active in these debates. Gifted and talented programs are very popular with parents. School leaders and local politicians are well aware of the value of these programs to people who are active in the schools and active in politics. The *New York Times* report by David Herszenhorn on February 17, 2005, would surprise almost no one involved in the world of education: "Acting on Mayor Michael R. Bloomberg's election-year promise to expand gifted and talented programs in the New York public schools, city education officials said yesterday that they would develop a standardized admissions test for such programs to be administered to 4- and 5-year-olds beginning in the spring of 2006." The New York City Schools are engaged in an old and empty venture.

WHAT COMES OF SEARCHES TO MEASURE "IT"?

The American history of education for the gifted or talented is a history of looking for standardized tests to identify children and youth as special as early as possible. We have had no success doing this. The measures we have been using simply do not seem to predict adult accomplishment.

And yet they must predict adult accomplishment, in order for the measures to be valid. As Gruber (1986) explains: "If the concept of gifted-ness is to be taken seriously, a gift must have as its consequence some connection with extraordinary achievement" (p. 261). If we cannot show predictive value for the measures we use to identify children and youth as in need of special services, how can we defend spending money or making any special provisions for this group? But there is no evidence that the hundreds and thousands of children and youth we have identified as gifted or talented over the last five or more decades, and for whom we have provided special educational services, have gone on to fill the ranks of the most talented or accomplished adults in our society.

Who Are the "Termites"? What Did They Do?

Terman's sample of "genius" youth—more than 1,000 California children with IQs above 140—followed from childhood well into adulthood, provides a most instructive case. The Terman longitudinal studies (*Genetic Studies of Genius*, 1925) were perhaps the first systematic studies demonstrating the difficulty of identifying potential. Many of the children and youth identified as genius at the start of the study did go on to realize meaningful adult accomplishments: The men in the group earned PhDs, medical degrees, and law degrees in numbers far greater than would be expected from any random group of an equivalent size, and were well published and credited with many patents (Getzels & Dillon, 1973, p. 697). But, as a group, the "Termites," as they were sometimes called, did not realize accomplishments anywhere as stellar as Terman or others initially had expected. Not all went to college; many had college records that were only fair to poor; many had careers much less distinguished than was anticipated by researchers at the time based on beliefs about the value of a high IQ score. As the genius children moved through the stages of life, they became more and more, well, ordinary. Or, as Sears (1979) put it when she looked at the data on Terman's group of genius youth 50 years later,

> Few of the thousands of variables measured in the gifted group show the homogeneity of the original IQ scores. Some, like education, income, and other demographic measures, do have skewed distributions with means

much higher than comparable data from unselected groups, but wide within-group variability is a prime characteristic of the sample. (p. 95)

Does High IQ Predict Outstanding Achievement?
If Not, Why Measure It?

When Subotnik, Kassan, Summers, and Wasser (1993) studied the adult lives of "grown-up high-IQ children from Hunter College Elementary School" (p. vii), it was a "school for the intellectually gifted" (p. 20) in New York City, serving students from nursery school to Grade 6 who entered with an IQ score of 130 or above (mean IQ 157). Again, this study reminds us how difficult it is to identify youth who will realize exceptional adult accomplishment, and how poorly IQ functions as a potential early indicator. As Subotnik and her colleagues report: "Although most of our study participants are successful and fairly content with their lives and accomplishments, there are no superstars, no Pulitzer Prize or MacArthur Award winners, and only one or two familiar names" (p. 11).

Prodigies and Discontinuities

Even scholars studying prodigies—children and youth with very specific talents who demonstrate their accomplishments in the youthful moment—find that, in the shift from childhood and youth to adulthood, early exceptional abilities may not forecast later achievements (Feldman, 1986; Goldsmith, 2000). As Goldsmith (2000) writes:

> By and large, the children I have studied have not gained national attention for their work, although they are still young enough that they may yet do so in the future. Some have long since given up their original areas of achievement, so if they are to develop national visibility, it will be in some other domain of accomplishment. (p. 115)

Simonton (2003) worries at length about what he calls the enigma of how not all of Terman's "genius" children made good, and how not all of Catharine Cox's (1926) "eminent adults" would have qualified for inclusion in Terman's study of gifted youth. Simonton points out that there are far more of these instances of missing connections from youth to adulthood than direct links between promise and accomplishment. But then he goes on to argue that

> with a better understanding of these developmental discontinuities, we may someday learn how to ensure that the more auspicious path becomes the norm rather than the exception. Perhaps all the subjects of a future longitudinal

study of gifted children will later qualify for inclusion in a subsequent retrospective study of genius adults. (p. 366)

In other words, he retains the belief that there are qualities we can identify in children that will mark who will achieve exceptional adult accomplishment; he believes we just have not found the linking qualities yet.

Of course it is possible to look at the same data—the discontinuities between those labeled gifted in their youth and those with outstanding accomplishments as adults—and arrive at different interpretations and conclusions. Perhaps we have been looking for talent in all the wrong places, or at all the wrong times. Perhaps the very act of labeling a child gifted or talented has negative consequences that outweigh any special educational attention the youth might receive.

LOOKING FOR TALENT IN THE WRONG PLACES OR AT THE WRONG TIMES

Are we looking for talent in all the wrong places or at all the wrong times? Motivation, persistence, commitment, stick-to-itiveness, perseverance, even interest—or any of the other qualities that signal some version of a sincere and long-term engagement with something—are seldom included as serious measures for identifying who is and who is not gifted or talented. Naturally, it is hard to figure how to include these forward-looking characteristics in any backward-looking measure. Yet in the 1980s the Bloom (1985) studies of the development of talent (about which we shall have much more to say shortly) and a variety of studies of expertise (e.g., Ericsson, Krampe, & Tesch-Romer, 1993), have been raising the question of whether persistence is the quality that trumps field-specific content attributes. This is not entirely a new hypothesis. Data in support of this contention can be found even in the Terman studies of genius.

Persistence Matters, a Lot

Lewis Terman undoubtedly did not expect persistence to matter so much at the start of his longitudinal studies. But he found that it mattered a great deal when, 18 years after the start of his classic study, he identified a group of his gifted youth who had "made use of their superior intellectual ability" and a group who were lower ranked in this regard. As Getzels and Dillon (1973) tell the story, the characteristics that distinguished the two groups "recall Galton's observations and those made by Cox (1926) in her study of historic genius: 'High but not the highest intelligence, combined with the greatest degree of persistence, will achieve greater eminence than the highest degree of intelligence with somewhat less persistence'" (Getzels & Dillon, pp. 697–698). Yet the question of who will be interested, who will be motivated to stay with a course of learning even during times of frustration or obvious lack of success, who will persist through the long-term course of developing talent, has been left behind for the past three quarters of a century as researchers have struggled with other qualities that have not served us well in linking youth with adult achievements.

Labels to Live Up To; Labels to Live Down

Are there negative consequences from labeling? There might be nothing wrong with the qualities we are using to identify gifted or talented youth except that the mere act of labeling may too often do more harm than good. Psychological research might help us think about the challenges we face helping children and youth learn something new or work at something more difficult than they have encountered before, if they already have been lauded and labeled as special for behavior that only an adult can know will likely be limiting in the long run.

Consider this concrete example: A young male tennis player can become champion in his age group by playing a better baseline tennis game than his peers. If he stays close to the baseline and retrieves everything that gets over the net, eventually his opponents will miss a return. But if the 8-year-old or 10-year-old persists in playing only a baseline game and hesitates to learn a serve-and-volley alternative because it is so difficult for youngsters with short legs and short arms, then in the long run the child will miss the transition from young phenom to adult talent. The child needs to do the hard work of learning to serve and volley when his body is not yet prepared to succeed. He will lose many matches. He will not look particularly remarkable. And he will need considerable help from parents and teachers to understand that winning, being the best in the moment, which may have been so rewarding for a number of years, needs to be sacrificed for long-term growth. But what if being gifted or talented matters too much to let go for however much time it takes to learn the new skills that will help with the transition from childhood extraordinariness to adult expertise?

Similarly, imagine the student who is quick and accomplished with arithmetic, who is rewarded for her speed with computation, suddenly facing mathematics that requires knowledge and skill quite different from computation. Is it not possible that this child will decide she has reached the limits of her talent or the limits of her interest in doing something when the rewards are no longer so forthcoming? As McNabb (2003) summarizes, "when gifted students are more focused on preserving their identity as 'gifted' than on increasing their competence, they may limit their potential by avoiding challenge" (p. 422).

Adult accomplishment turns out to hinge on a great deal more than identifying and then supporting youth who demonstrate exceptionality at something vaguely related to adult activity.

MORE DYNAMIC WAYS OF THINKING ABOUT TALENT AND ITS DEVELOPMENT

In recent years we have seen a move afoot to understand talent differently, to understand it in a way that may actually make a significant difference for children and youth and for society. The change is represented in work by Benjamin Bloom (1985), and, succinctly, in a conclusion he drew at the end of his 5-year study of the development of talent.

Bloom's research team studied groups of individuals who, though relatively young (under the age of 35), had realized exceptional levels of adult accomplishment in one of six fields: concert piano, sculpture, swimming, tennis, mathematics, and research neurology (two artistic disciplines, two psychomotor activities, and two academic/intellectual fields). The project explored the lives of 120 talented individuals in all, approximately 20 in each field. At the start of the project, Bloom held the expectation that the individuals studied "would be initially identified as possessing special gifts or qualities and then provided with special instruction and encouragement" (Bloom, 1982, p. 520) as a result of these gifts or qualities. But the data from the study made it clear that his initial assumption of early discovery followed by instruction and support was wrong (Bloom, 1985, 1982).

Despite the considerable adult achievements of the individuals in the sample for the Development of Talent Research Project, as children they typically did *not* show unusual promise at the start. And typically, there was no early intention of working toward a standard of excellence in a particular field. Instead of early discovery followed by development, the researchers found quite consistently that the individuals were encouraged and supported in considerable learning—often informal but also formal—before they were identified as special and accorded even more encouragement and support. More time and interest invested in the talent field resulted in further identification of special qualities that in turn were again rewarded with more encouragement and support. Aptitudes, attitudes, and expectations grew in concert with one another and were mutually confirming (Sosniak, 1985).

THE SHIFT FROM INNATE CHARACTERISTIC
TO ALTERABLE VARIABLE

And so it came to be that Bloom faced findings he did not expect, findings even that were counter to what he had predicted at the start of his study. And in the best tradition of scholarship, he was able to change his world-view. He told a reporter: "We were looking for exceptional kids and what we found were exceptional conditions" (Carlson, 1985, p. 49).

In Bloom's work, we see the idea of talent shift from an innate characteristic to an alterable variable. Talent was no longer something one had, something that might blossom or be wasted; talent was something one could develop. The idea of talent became organized in some significant measure around effort and persistence. Talent could be created, produced, grown. Rather than being limited by some God-given characteristics, rather than being rare or extraordinary, talent became possible for very large numbers of children and youth.

Bloom promoted the shift of talent from innate characteristic to alterable variable for two reasons. First, in his research studies he was unable to find the innate qualities or characteristics that would help identify talent early in childhood, try as he might. And he did try, although, admittedly, he was limited by the retrospective nature of his studies. Second, the data his team collected told a story again and again and again of a long-term development of talent. An absolutely critical variable for individuals in the Bloom studies became commitment to a talent area over a long time, persistence, stick-to-itiveness, motivation, willingness to persevere even in the face of periods of failure. Hints from the Terman studies about the importance of perseverance became shouts from the Bloom studies.

Motivating Persistence

In recent years there has been increasing agreement that the central challenge of helping people develop exceptional abilities is that of creating and maintaining the motivation necessary to stay with a field for the many years it takes to develop expertise. Even if we are able, someday, to identify innate characteristics helpful for exceptional development of one sort or another, these characteristics are likely to account for only a very small amount of a person's ultimate accomplishments. Thus the central challenge for studies of the development of talent becomes: How do we create and maintain conditions that support student perseverance over the long term?

The Bloom studies pose some hints of what might be required. These studies point, for example, to changing motivations and changing supports over the long periods of time studying and becoming expert in a particular field. The long-term process of developing talent was not simply a matter of becoming quantitatively more knowledgeable and skilled over time, or of working more intensely for longer hours. It was, predominantly, a matter of qualitative and evolutionary transformations. The individuals were transformed, the substance of what was being learned was transformed, and the manner in which individuals engaged with teachers and field-specific content was transformed. Students progressively adopted different views of who they were, of what their fields of expertise were about, and of how the field fitted into their lives (Sosniak, 1987). These transformations generally followed a pattern reminiscent of Whitehead's (1929) rhythms of learning—phases of romance, precision, and generalization—over the course of their long years of work in their respective fields.

Insights from Whitehead's Phases of Learning

Whitehead's phases of learning, and Bloom's findings, can be summarized this way. The first phase of learning—the phase of romance—is an extended period of playfulness, exploration, and novelty with small but immediate rewards and encouragement. The primary concern in this period is setting in motion possibilities, getting the learner involved, captivated, perhaps even hooked on further learning. Once a learner is involved, invested, there is a necessary transition to the second phase of learning—the phase of precision. During this second period of learning the central concern is with technical mastery and intellectual development, with learning the rules and exceptions of the language of the field. Students and teachers pay considerable attention to details and vocabulary, and to judging an individual's own competence in relation to the competence of others more expert. The third phase of learning—the phase of generalization—is a return to the playfulness of the phase of romance with the added advantage of significant knowledge and skill. Now students learn to shed details in favor of the application of broader principles; they give considerable attention to personal involvement and expression and to inventing and cutting new pathways. The set of phases are dependent not on age but on experience and on the development of aptitudes and attitudes; they also appear to be iterative, and the process repeats as tasks and demands in a field change.

   Bloom's studies also point to the power of engaging children and youth with tasks and tools that connect their learning to the lives lead by adults in society who also were engaged with the specific talent area. Children and youth used materials that are part of our social technologies—they played pianos that adults used also, they learned music that they knew adults played and listened to; they swam in Olympic-sized pools; they read field-specific books and magazines that were created for the consuming public. Children and youth engaged in adjudications, competitions, and science fairs doing work they knew adults who were invested in the field did also. The children and youth had occasion to see adults doing the same tasks they were doing with the same tools they were using—on television; through magazines, books, and recordings; and sometimes in person. Both the tasks the youth engaged in and the materials they used to pursue their tasks were connected to tasks valued by significant portions of society. And youth knew these tasks and materials were valued because they saw them being displayed by others in their family, in their community, and in ever larger arenas.

Communities of Practice: Social Contexts for Growing Talent

Following from this, Bloom's studies pointed again and again to the power of the social context for helping create and sustain motivation to learn over the long term. One of the most obvious lessons from the Development of Talent Research Project was that no one develops talent on his or her own, without the support, encouragement, advice, insight, guidance, and good-will of many others. The development of talent as it was unveiled in the Bloom studies was a tribute of many people working for the accomplishments of one.

The many years of work on the way to international recognition involved increasing exposure to and participation in communities of practice for the respective talent fields. These communities of practice offered not only models for development but also resources for support, inspiration, and sustenance. Communities of practice created standards for work—for work by the novice, the knowledgeable layman, and the expert. At their best, communities of practice modeled and inspired excellence, they defined and gave meaning to significant educative tasks, and they supported and sustained work over the long periods necessary for the development of talent. The youth and young adults in the Development of Talent Research Project were fortunate to be invited into, or to find their way into, communities that shaped and inspired their work. They had many varied opportunities to see themselves as members of field-specific communities, to come to know the commitments, and to watch and live out for themselves the process of a community renewing itself.

A need for understanding the significant long-term process for the development of talent was becoming apparent even before the Bloom studies. Cognitive scientists like Simon and Chase (1973) called attention to the long process of learning in their study of chess expertise, research Bloom drew on for his own work. Some years after the Bloom studies, Ericsson and colleagues (1993) would pull together many studies telling the same story about learning over the long term.

Of course a long-term process for the development of talent does not negate the possibility that there also may be innate characteristics that, under the right circumstances, might make a real difference for developing exceptional levels of talent. But it does seem that right now we are far from being able to identify important innate characteristics. And most important, whatever the characteristics of children and youth that we might learn to identify, it seems unlikely that these characteristics will supplant the necessity for a long-term process of learning.

HERE'S WHERE OUR CONVERSATION STARTS: THE ACADEMIC TALENT DEVELOPMENT PROGRAM

In a context where giftedness and talent may or may not mean different things (general versus specific; potential versus accomplishment), where early identification of youth who will go on to realize exceptional adult achievement has proved futile, and where long-term commitment to learning seems at least a necessary if not sufficient condition for developing talent, the directors of the Academic Talent Development Program have had to make decisions about the educational program they would offer.

As noted in the introduction, the earliest version of today's ATDP began in 1981 when the first director decided to affiliate with the Johns Hopkins Academic Talent Search Program. The UC Berkeley Gifted Program, as it was called then, was a West Coast version of the Johns Hopkins program, which had been created and run for many years by Julian Stanley. Johns Hopkins University and UC Berkeley had (and have) a great deal in common as academic institutions, and it was not yet quite so obvious that early identification, or talent searches, were likely to have so little long-term payoff.

Gradually, as the program developed at Berkeley, program staff grew uneasy with the talent search orientation. It did not seem to meet the needs and interests of youth and parents in the Bay Area. And it was out of line with the growing body of research on the development of talent. The staff did some careful study on what might be offered and how the program could defend different offerings. Then the focus of the program changed from searching for giftedness to developing talent.

What's Talent in the ATDP Context?

Talent, for the Academic Talent Development Program, has a very specific meaning. The program staff recognize an extremely wide range of talents, but choose to focus this summer program only on talent associated with academic work. In ATDP, one can develop talent in the natural sciences, such as biology, physics, chemistry, engineering, and so on. One can develop talent in the humanities, such as writing, literature, and languages. There are possibilities for talent development in the social sciences and the arts. The academic world is large enough to allow for the development of many talents; in a single program it did not seem necessary or desirable to go beyond this portfolio.

The choice to focus on specific academic talents seems almost self-evident in retrospect, but it was not so obvious at the start, and many programs still do not take this orientation. There are various programs invested in talent or giftedness much more generally; these are typically programs that focus on creativity, leadership, problem solving, or critical thinking.

For ATDP, the focus on specific academic talents allows for an extremely tight fit between the site offering the program (UC Berkeley) and the substance of the program. The setting thus can send its own multiple consistent messages about the nature and value of academic talent to the ATDP youth. And how is the value of academic talent communicated? Here is one example: The only reserved faculty automobile parking on the Berkeley campus, in the best located parking spaces, belongs to Nobel Prize winners. The "Nobel" spots are prominently labeled, they are sometimes an item on the traditional ATDP scavenger hunts, and they generate comment from many ATDP students who pass the parking spots as they walk across campus on the way to or from class.

Developing a Talent for Developing Talents, Not Searching for Giftedness

From hindsight it seems that the director and staff were creating a program to support youth in a life that the adults guiding the program all lived and valued. They were creating a program that might help develop more people just like themselves: people engaged with and fascinated by academic knowledge and ideas. The staff were not entirely self-conscious early on that they wanted to build a community that was interested and interesting in the ways that they were themselves. But that is very much what happened. The ATDP community would share an enthusiasm for the academic disciplines, for playing with and arguing over knowledge and ideas, for wondering about how their local world and the larger universe worked. The director and staff were working at a great university, they valued that environment, and they hoped to communicate the excitement of that environment to students motivated to join the program for a summer.

The clear focus on developing talent rather than searching for gifted-ness did not remove the challenge of how to deal with individual differ-ences. Respect for individual differences remained important to the staff, although in a very different form than at the start. No one working with the program has ever doubted for a moment that there are individual dif-ferences among children and youth. The question the program has grappled with was what differences to treat most seriously.

The differences the UC Berkeley Gifted Program had first taken most seriously were norm-referenced differences as revealed on standardized tests of academic aptitude. But increasingly it seemed that these were not differences that truly matter for the long run. The program staff thought seriously about R. S. Peters's (1967) argument that "distinctions should be made if there are relevant differences and . . . they should not be made if there are no relevant differences or on the basis of irrelevant differences" (p. 51). The director and staff pondered whether speed and power on a standardized academic aptitude test were relevant for the development of specific academic talents. They had to consider whether being some small or large amount better than others the same age on a norm-referenced test unlinked to actual behaviors was a relevant difference.

The director and staff decided that speed and power on some stan-dardized norm-referenced aptitude test were not relevant differences for ATDP. And although there are obviously quite a few innate differences among children and youth, some of which might even be talent-specific, it was not clear what difference the innate characteristics made for the lives people create for themselves. Two distinctions among youth did seem to vastly outweigh all others in importance for developing talent: (a) the de-sire to learn and (b) the desire to learn about something specific. Thus the individual differences the program chose to honor were differences in motivation and differences in field-specific interests.

Growing a Passion for Learning

The application process thus needed to determine motivation and to de-termine field-specific interests. As described elsewhere in this book, we believe it does both of those things. Applying is not a trivial process; it requires a great deal of work. And, in the course of applying, students must make their own decisions about what would be worth studying. The stu-dents decide what they think is worth their time and effort, and ATDP aims to support the students' choices.

ATDP is different. It begins with a premise that the work of the program is to create talent, build it, grow it, develop it—certainly not to seek to mine or unearth it. Following from this, ATDP defines for its constituency the specific talents it is designed to promote, and creates conditions that, it hopes, will support children and youth who are interested in one of these areas and willing to work hard (at least for one or more summers). ATDP aims to make the academic language, the conversation, and the work seductive.

ATDP has taken the road less traveled for extracurricular talent programs. Programs around the country still search for potential. They still use norm-referenced measures (most often measures of general achievement or aptitude rather than specific talents) to decide who to include and who to exclude. They still offer general courses that may or may not be related to students' specific interests or to any adult specific area of accomplishment.

THE DO-IT-YOURSELF GIFTED PROGRAM

A friendly faculty colleague at Berkeley, Rhona Weinstein, has called ATDP the only do-it-yourself gifted program in the world: "Want to be gifted? Come here and we'll help you learn how." ATDP makes a conscious effort to attend to what an education program can do to enhance an interested student's academic talents, without worrying for a moment about whether the student would be considered talented by virtue of some innate criteria, norm-referenced or otherwise.

Nor do the program staff worry about how far their students will travel. As the director of the program is fond of saying to parents of ATDP students, "Your children are not going to be doctors—at least not right now. Right now they are going to be eighth graders or ninth graders or tenth graders. And these years need to be lived richly, filled with tasks and challenges worthwhile in their own right, ripe with opportunities to develop interests and talents."

If someday a former ATDP student were to win a Nobel Prize, the program staff certainly would crow. But the goals they focus on are quite different. The staff look forward to students stopping by the program office and spontaneously talking about something they just learned and found interesting. They rejoice when a teenager asks *how* to learn something and means it. They believe they have done a good job when they see an application from a returning student interested in learning more. They smile inwardly when their students report—in person or on annual evaluation forms—that work at ATDP is harder than any school work they have ever encountered and that fact is one of the great things about the program. They treasure the unsolicited letters they receive from alumni and their parents reporting on what has happened since ATDP and reflecting on the ATDP experience.

NEARLY TWENTY YEARS AS ATDP:
SO WHAT HAVE WE LEARNED?

For more than 16 years now, the program has been called the Academic Talent Development Program. Giftedness is gone from the program name and the underlying program plan. All written material has been clear about the program purposes, about who ATDP might serve, and about how ATDP might serve those children and youth. Of course the audience for the program—the youth who attend and the parents who support their participation—has not had the same period of study and reflection on education for the gifted and talented as had the ATDP staff before they changed their orientation from a search for gifted students to a program for developing talent. When parents and children first encounter ATDP they bring ideas they have developed on the street about the requirements and expectations of such programs. At least some of the parents of ATDP youth know about GATE (gifted and talented education) programs offered by public schools in the area; undoubtedly they transfer some understandings about those programs to ATDP as well.

One of the frequently asked questions, in telephone calls and e-mail to the ATDP office, a question asked so frequently that it has earned a place in the program catalog, goes like this: "I have not been identified as 'gifted' by my school. Is this program appropriate for me?" The written answer in the brochure reads this way: "Official school designation of 'gifted' is not required for admission. Instead, students should be hardworking, enjoy learning, and be prepared for an intellectually stimulating and demanding summer class."

Thus we must ask the question about whether the program participants have self-selected, have created an old-fashioned gifted and talented program by their own decisions about whether to apply. Despite all the serious program development and outreach by the ATDP staff, are the students who take part essentially the same students who would have been part of any gifted and talented program in the state or the country? Who does come, and how does the director know that all the program deliberations about who to serve have had any consequence? Let us begin to answer these questions by looking at how successful ATDP students stack up in relation to the traditional gifted and talented concerns about scores on norm-referenced standardized tests of aptitude or achievement.

As we said in the introduction, ATDP was less diverse and more exclusive in the summer of 1990, when it was still in the process of moving away from searching for gifted students and toward the growing of academic talent. For that year, 61% of the 673 students scored at or above the

90th percentile on the verbal portion of a standardized test, and 77% scored at or above the 90th percentile on the math portion of a standardized test.

In contrast, by the summer of 1996, when the program was more fully established as one that developed academic talent, the program was more diverse. To put it another way, in 1996, 45% of the 999 students in ATDP scored in the 90th percentile or above on the verbal portion of a norm-referenced standardized achievement test, and 55% of the students scored in the 90th percentile or above on the math portion of a norm-referenced standardized achievement test: These students would very likely qualify for many a gifted and talented program. The other half of the ATDP student population likely would have been excluded from almost every gifted and talented program by virtue of their lower rankings on the traditional admissions tests.

The pattern of test scores appeared largely the same for 1996 and 2002, while the enrollment had increased by 124 students. For example, in 2002, with an enrollment of 1,023, 15.5% of students scored at or above the 97% in both the verbal and mathematics portions of a norm-referenced standardized test. In 1996, at 999 students, that number had been 15.6%. For 1996 and 2002 respectively, 5.9% and 8% of students reported verbal test scores between the 40th–59th percentiles; 5.7% and 4.6% reported verbal scores less than the 40th percentile.

Looking at the data for these two points, we believe we see a program that seems stabilized in its student population relative to achievement test scores. About half of the students ATDP serves, maybe somewhat more than half, would be considered too low-scoring to merit attention by most of the gifted and talented programs in the country. These students would not have been entitled to try to develop academic talent because they would be considered unqualified or not competitive by virtue of their scores on a standardized test of verbal or mathematical abilities.

ATDP students are also diverse in many ways besides test scores. For example, in the summer of 1993, nearly 30% of ATDP students came from homes with annual family incomes that ranged, for a family of four, from below the poverty line to barely above it, with these students qualifying for a free or reduced-cost lunch. Father's education for this group of ATDP students included 11% of fathers with, at most, a high school diploma or its equivalent. Another 16.5% had some education past high school, but had not earned a 4-year college degree. Mother's education included 13% with, at most, a high school diploma or its equivalent, and nearly 23% more with some education past high school but not a 4-year college degree. The rest of the parents had BA degrees or higher. At ATDP, children of farm workers learn side by side with children whose parents own vineyards and children whose parents and grandparents own film studios and have won Academy Awards.

A diverse group of students sit side by side in class, but do they stand side by side in success with the academic conversation? Do they succeed similarly, and do they hold similar (and positive) attitudes toward the program? We believe so. And we will provide evidence that it is possible to serve well a population that is diverse in its standardized test scores, diverse in its home experience with formal education, diverse in its economic status, and diverse in its academic interests. Before we offer evidence about the consequences of the program, it seems important to share a lot more about what happens for 6 weeks summer after summer. The next chapter tells more of that story.

Welcome to the
Academic Conversation!

THE THEME FOR THE STORY we will tell in the pages that follow is "welcoming youth into the academic conversation." We take this theme from Mike Rose's (1989) *Lives on the Boundary*. Rose's story is about "America's educational underclass." Ours is about the development of academic talent. Notwithstanding the considerable differences in the students Rose wrote about and many of those ATDP serves, we believe there is much in common with the work we do with youth in the service of developing academic talent.

> Nothing is more exclusive than the academic club: its language is highbrow, it has fancy badges, and it worships tradition. It limits itself to a few participants who prefer to talk to each other. What Father Albertson did was bring us inside the circle, nudging us out into the chatter, always just behind us, whispering to try this step, then this one, encouraging us to feel the moves for ourselves. (p. 58)

ATDP aims to do with about 2,400 students each year what Rose himself experienced. The ATDP plan for developing academic talent is guided in no small measure by research on the development of talent both in and outside of school. We know, for example, that one of the significant aspects of the development of all sorts of talents is the long-term nature of the talent development process (see for example Bloom, 1985; Ericsson et al., 1993). The development of academic talent is not an objective we can set out to achieve quickly. But the program can welcome students into the conversation and help them pursue it and persist at it. And, following Rose, the program can help youth see what a particular kind of talk would enable them to do:

> [My teachers] liked books and ideas, and they liked to talk about them in ways that fostered growth rather than established dominance. They lived their knowledge. And maybe because of that their knowledge grew in me in ways that led back out to the world. I was developing a set of tools with which to shape a life. (Rose, 1989, p. 58)

ONE MORE ADVANTAGE FOR SOME; FOR OTHERS, IT'S MUCH MORE SIGNIFICANT

Mike Rose's account was particularly focused on the educational under-class. And for this group he writes:

> To live your early life on the streets of South L.A.—or Homewood or Span-ish Harlem or Chicago's South Side or any one of hundreds of other depressed communities—and to journey up through the top levels of the American educational system will call for support and guidance at many, many points along the way. You'll need people to guide you into conversations that seem foreign and threatening. You'll need models, lots of them, to show you how to get at what you don't know. You'll need people to help you center your-self in your own developing ideas. You'll need people to watch out for you. (pp. 47–48)

We believe that Mike Rose was close in his assessment, but not quite right. It is not only youth from depressed communities that need people to guide them and show them and help them and watch out for them. The "journey up through the top levels of the American educational system" calls for support and guidance for all youth. Some youth find support and guidance at home, from their extended families, from their neighbors, even in the streets—the educated streets—they inhabit. And some youth need ATDP more than others, because their lived worlds are not as fully infused with academic models and knowledgeable insiders. ATDP offers support and guidance and models for all who make the first telephone call to the program or the first visit to its Web page. For some students, the ATDP environment is just one more advantage on the journey toward academic accomplishment; for others, ATDP is much more significant.

WELCOME TO THE ACADEMIC CLUB!

ATDP meets youth relatively early in the long-term process of talent de-velopment: Its Elementary Division begins with students who have just completed kindergarten; its Secondary Division begins with students who have just completed Grade 7. It meets them at a point where the program might "provoke young people to develop a sense of oughtness, to think . . . about the kinds of human beings they would like to be" (Greene, 1989, p. 9). Greene argues that "people are more likely to . . . choose or to adopt standards if they see themselves as members of a community marked by certain commitments and always in the process of renewing itself" (p. 11). ATDP works purposefully to help youth chose to become members of academic communities, and to encourage them to adopt as their own the standards of a scholarly life in the sciences, mathematics, or the humanities. It brings them into the club and assists them in becoming active and dedicated members.

TRADITIONS FROM THE FIRST MEETING SET THE TONE

On the morning of June 12, 2004, children and their parents filled the 800-seat auditorium in Wheeler Hall on the campus of the University of California at Berkeley. There were so many they had to come in shifts: Those with last names beginning A–K were scheduled for 9:00–10:30; last names beginning L–Z were to come from 11:00–12:30. But even with two shifts, Wheeler Hall was overflowing. The orientation was for students in the Secondary Division of ATDP, typically youth between the ages of 12 and 17, and their parents. Whole families came. Older youth who had taken part in previous years came to pass the baton. Younger children, infants and toddlers even, were there, in strollers, in parents' arms, sitting on parents' laps.

The atmosphere was enthusiastic. Families who knew one another from past summers with the program greeted each other cheerfully outside of the university building and inside its halls. Students shared gossip about who else was coming this summer, and what they knew about students who had graduated or otherwise moved on.

They came for the orientation of the Academic Talent Development Program, held each summer for 6 weeks on the university campus. Had they come because they were interested in academic talent development? Were they there because it was a summer program run by UC Berkeley? Were they there because, given the options, it was a relatively inexpensive way to provide some organization to the long school break? Frankly, we can't be sure. Probably different families were drawn for each of those reasons, and for many more.

Everything Here Is Purposeful—and Complex

We do know, as they knew, that there would be nothing easy about the program that would begin in less than 2 weeks. It was not easy even to apply. The students were required to select one course for the summer from a program book that resembles a college catalog. They were required to get a recommendation from a current teacher, on a form provided by the program. They were required to include a photocopy of their most recent report card with their application, and a report of their scores from the most recent standardized achievement test they had taken at school. They were required to outline their interests and activities in and outside of school. They were required to submit a piece of work they had completed in the past school year or write a well-developed essay of no more than 1,500 words on one of two topics provided. They were required to sign a Statement of Commitment: "I understand that students may be dismissed from the Program without refund because of two or more absences, failure to complete assignments, or behavior unfitting to the purpose of the Program." A parent or guardian also had to sign in agreement with the commitment. All this just to apply to the program, just to earn an invitation to join the club. And still they persisted.

WHAT BRINGS YOU HERE TODAY? A VOLKSWAGEN PHAETON

That Saturday in Wheeler Hall three students spoke about past years' experiences with the program. They spoke with the affect and humor of teenagers. Carolina, now a college student, told how she talked her family into letting her come to the program as a 12-year-old almost 10 years before. They thought she was too young to be on the Berkeley campus alone, so they insisted she could come only if her older sister went also. "I wanted to make sure that I never had to take a class with my older sister. So I selected only the very hardest classes. I knew I'd never see her there."

Tom, a student in his ninth summer with the program, told this story recalling his very first summer experience with the Elementary Division of the program.

> I still remember my first course, right after first grade. Greek Mythology. . . . As an example of how the knowledge you gain here will stay with you and aid you so far into the future, consider this: Volkswagen is making a new luxury sedan called the Phaeton. In my first class at ATDP I learned that Phaeton was the son of the god Apollo who killed himself (he pauses here for emphasis) when he crashed his father's celestial chariot. Someone at VW didn't do their homework.

The audience exploded in laughter. And then, just a beat later, Tom added, "But I did." And, if it was possible, the laughter was even louder.

The students on stage that morning talked about how much they had learned, how competent they felt academically, how confident they felt in situations that might overwhelm others their age either intellectually or socially. Each, in his or her own way, spoke about having met "so many different people from so many different backgrounds, economically and racially." Carolina asked aloud the question of what her summers would have been like without ATDP. And then she answered it. "I would not have been *exposed*," she said—"exposed to people, to the idea of college, to excitement for learning."

During the 6-week summer program the students and their teachers spread across the UC-Berkeley campus, from Barker Hall on the west to Latimer Hall on the east, from Tolman Hall (home to the Graduate School of Education) on the north, to Dwinelle Hall on the south. But on this day everyone gathered in Wheeler Hall, and the size and diversity of the program was on display.

THE ACADEMIC CONVERSATION AND THE WORK BEGIN IMMEDIATELY

After the various talks to the large group, and after all the teachers had walked on stage and introduced themselves, the students and their parents headed for the designated location in Wheeler Hall where they would meet with their particular teacher. The Secondary Division of ATDP offers approximately 40 different courses, many with multiple sections resulting in more than 80 classes, distributed across six departments (Writing and Literature, Languages, Computer Science, Mathematics, Social Sciences, and Natural Sciences). So today it takes three floors of the large university building to accommodate them in small groups. The main floor, the second floor, and the basement corridors were lined with bright orange and green signs indicating the teachers' names, course numbers, and course names.

Here in the corridors we see the process of learning start to be played out. Under the orange and green signs, students and their teachers huddled in groups, talking about the course, the required books and where they could be purchased, and any questions the students and parents had. Teachers made certain to welcome each student personally. While parents chatted and shared plans with each other about transportation for the summer, students received an introductory letter from the teacher, which included the assignment due on the first day of class.

From the First Introduction, Learning Is Made Personal

ATDP students have homework to do even before the first day of class— serious homework, such as completing exercises in preparation for learning *hiragana* and *katakana* syllabaries for Japanese class, writing a mathematics autobiography, attempting some of the instructor's favorite math problems, or familiarizing themselves with pages of legal terms for the Practice of Law course. These letters, in which the teacher introduces himself or herself and introduces the course, are part of the director's expectation for each class. But the director does not read the notes the teachers write before these notes are hand delivered to the students at the orientation or mailed to those who could not attend that meeting.

The notes are intended to be a personal invitation from a teacher to his or her students, reflecting the individual teacher and the specific course. As individual as the welcome notes are, any group of them also reveals the nature and intentions of the program: "We are serious about this"; "We can't wait to get started"; "This will be different from anything you have ever experienced in school." Across any set of notes one can feel the passion of the teachers for their subject matter and their students.

Here is one such letter in its entirety. It was written by Deena G., for the students in her class on Intermediate Writing. The class, scheduled for Tuesdays and Fridays from 8:30 to noon, was set to begin 10 days later, the second day of the summer program.

> Dear Students,
>
> Welcome to Intermediate Writing. In this class we will be exploring the relationship between identity (yours, mine! those of the other writers we will be reading) and writing, identity and the language(s) we speak, and identity and the stories we tell (or don't tell). We will be reading and analyzing contemporary poems, essays, autobiography, and fiction by authors who are concerned with these issues, and you will have the chance to experiment with these authors' ideas, writing styles, and strategies in your own writing.
>
> Before coming to our first meeting, I would like you to read Gloria Anzaldua's "How to Tame a Wild Tongue." (It's the first entry in your course reader.) In this essay, Anzaldua argues that we *are* the languages we speak, that "ethnic identity is twin skin to linguistic identity." Do you agree? Consider the language(s) you speak, and how they relate to, or fail to relate to, your (ethnic) identity. Please write a 1–2 page response to Anzaldua's essay and the ideas she presents. You don't need to type this response, and you may write it as informally as you wish.
>
> I have attached a handout that I hope will give you a sense for the course's structure and the work it will involve. However, the main thing I'd like to tell you is that I want to give you lots of room in this course to play (you might think of this course as "How to

Free a Tame(d) Tongue"), to gain confidence in yourself as writers, and to develop a sense of the importance and purpose writing has for you.

I'm looking forward to our first class meeting on June 22 and, in the meantime, please give me a call and say hello sometime before class begins. Consider this part of your first assignment. (Also: I would like you to call me Deena. It makes me very nervous to be addressed as Ms. Garrison!) My phone number is ——. I can't wait to hear from you.

Substance Matters for Right Now and for the Future

Why so much fuss about the content of welcome letters? Because substance matters. Following the research on the development of talent and expertise, ATDP is self-conscious about offering subject-specific opportunities for learning. Studies of expert performance reveal again and again the importance of considerable exposure to domain-specific content in order to be able to reason insightfully, creatively, and productively in a particular arena (e.g., see Glaser & Chi, 1988). Teaching creative thinking or problem solving or leadership absent a body of knowledge within which to develop and use those skills simply won't do. Or, as Duckworth (1987) has put it,

> Intelligence cannot develop without matter to think about. Making new connections depends on knowing enough about something in the first place to provide the basis for thinking of other things to do—of other questions to ask—that demand more complex connections in order to make sense. The more ideas about something people already have at their disposal, the more new ideas occur and the more they can coordinate to build up still more complicated schemes. (p. 14)

Youth learn sense making in each task, assignment, and conversation, and each interaction helps build their store of new ideas and new combinations of already held ideas. It is in this context that ATDP youth hear the message about college expectations in each course at each session. Sometimes it is explicit, but most often it is implicit, embedded in the tasks they are asked to engage with and the pace at which they are asked to work.

Learning to Be an (Informed) Academic Risk Taker

Youth learn to behave in ways that will prepare them for college, whether or not they are completely aware of this. For example, they learn about intellectual risk taking:

Welcome to Dynamic Chemistry! Throughout this course the laboratory activities and discussions will focus on how chemists describe matter and its changes. Understanding the periodic table and the particulate nature of matter will provide the basis for us to think about the world in terms of particles and their interactions. This model will provide insight into what we observe in our daily lives and will provide the foundation necessary to predict, explain, and quantify changes in matter in order to problem-solve successfully. . . .

Beyond the mechanics, be ready to share what you are thinking and be able to explain your reasoning. I value what you are thinking as you are learning just as much as I value your achieving the right answer. This means that you will be taking risks to explain your thinking before you may already "know." This will be part of the adventure and I want you to be comfortable with this expectation.

Dynamic Chemistry

Kim D.

It's All Authentic, and Devoid of Easy Answers

And as Advanced Placement (AP) Psychology instructor Trisha B. makes clear in her first assignment, this is serious academic work we are setting out together to tackle. Her implication is that questions posed in class are authentic, complex, and have no easy answers—she wouldn't waste her students time by posing any other kind.

> The question "Do I exist?" is arguably the most difficult to prove or disprove, and has endured in some philosophical circles since ancient times. As psychology's historical roots are in the discipline of philosophy, you are to delve into this bewildering problem by writing a brief essay arguing that you either do or do not exist.
>
> Consider the following questions: Do you exist? How do you know? What evidence do you have that you exist (or do not exist)? What arguments would you use to support the claim?
>
> Also, consider what assumptions you need to make in order to argue your case. An *assumption* is a nonverified statement, something taken for granted or accepted as true without explicit supporting empirical evidence. A fundamental goal of science is to reduce the number of assumptions in any theory. Try to identify which of your statements are verified and which are assumptions you need to make in order for the argument to work.

While the Work Is Intense, So Is the Support

Clearly, the work expectations at ATDP are high. And so too are the expectations that teachers will support their students in meeting the course challenges. This is different from "school," as far too many of our youth know it. ATDP teachers are passionate. The subject matter is serious. The work expectations are high. As the following example shows, the support for students is considerable and readily available.

> You should expect 6–10 hours of homework for each class session. Please plan your time so that the homework is completed in 3 to 5 small blocks of time. Don't try to finish all of it in just one sitting.
>
> Studying with a friend or a group is a good way for everyone to be more successful. . . .
>
> . . . If you need help at night while doing your homework you may give me a call and I'll work with you to answer your questions. My hotline hours are ——. If I'm not at home you may leave a message on my recorder and I'll get back to you as soon as possible. My telephone number is ——. My email address is ——.
>
> Algebra 1
> Katie C.

Resources Come Right Along with Expectations

ATDP teachers are self-conscious about the academic expectations and aspirations they are trying to communicate. Recall the messages we shared earlier from the teachers' welcome letters, rich with university language, university requirements, and university work that students are expected to handle. Here, an example from the Practice of Law instructor:

> Inasmuch as this course will cover materials that might normally be discussed only in a graduate-level program (law school), it is quite natural that you may feel some apprehension over the course's content and methodology. I wish to assure you that, while we will be discussing actual (albeit selected) law school subjects, you should find the scope and pacing of the course to be comfortable and appropriate. . . .
>
> The book assigned is *Gilbert's Law Summary on Torts*. Additionally, I ask that you bring to class a copy of the United States Constitution. . . .
>
> Finally, I want to assure you that I will gladly be available to hear your questions, comments, and concerns regarding the class;

please feel free to telephone me at any reasonable hour at my home number ——. I have every confidence that you will find this course to be an enjoyable as well as educational experience, and I look forward eagerly to seeing you on June 19th. . . .

The Practice of Law
Howard L.

Welcome to Deep Subject Matter at the University

It is in class—in the actual teaching and learning—that the more subtle but also more substantial aspects of college are taught day after day. Students encounter content that touches areas they never reach in their middle school or secondary school classes. They encounter ways of learning—including the power of students working and studying together, and the possibility of resources for learning outside of the classroom—that are out of the ordinary, for the most part, in their academic-year school experiences. They learn that there is value in taking initiative, in being disciplined, in developing goals, and holding oneself responsible for meeting them. And they face a pace that, well, matches the pace of work in college courses on campus during the academic year; in other words, it is relentless.

The Tapestry of Mathematics is an enrichment class, intended for advanced students who are passionate about mathematics. So passionate that most had never had their mettle tested in their previous classes because they were always so well prepared for class. Their instructor, a PhD graduate in theoretical mathematics, was about to assume his first professorship in logic and philosophy. He prepared his students for what was to come this way:

> The good news: Tests and quizzes have little to do with the practice of real mathematics, so this course will avoid them. Here's the bad news: Real mathematics involves hours of frustration, requiring you to work on problems that you don't know how to solve, or even where to start. It involves carrying problems around for a while, waiting for inspiration to hit. Finally, it requires a serious level of commitment, and that's what is expected of you in this course.
> Edward R.

In her ATDP advanced writing class, Elena Z., also a freshman writing instructor at the university, lets her students know what the expectations are for their course, and at the same time alerts them to requirements they will revisit when they enter college. Through word and deed, the instructor shows her students that the class is as tough as it seems, and that she is present to support them as they meet the successive challenges:

> Students taking reading and composition courses at UC Berkeley (which usually go by the course numbers 1A or 1B) are required to produce at least 32 pages of written work to receive credit. If you add up the number of pages required for the essays for this class, you will get a range of 14 to 21 pages. Therefore, in order to get as much writing practice as you would in an English 1A course, we will write *at least* one page in class daily, in the form of journals, study questions, or creative pieces. *Please save all your written work in a folder or notebook.* Your notebook provides proof of the work you do. I will want to see it again at the end of the course—and you'll want to keep it after that, especially if you receive credit for this class.

THERE'S ALWAYS MORE HAPPENING THAN MEETS AN UNINFORMED EYE

In a folklore class students learn to think differently about everyday experiences, and they learn that scholars at a university do, indeed, take everyday experiences seriously:

> The jokes you tell, the stories you hear, many of the games you play—these cultural expressions likely are folklore. In this class we will study what is and what is not folklore, who are and who are not considered the folk. . . . As young folklorists, you will begin to collect folklore from your family and friends. You will learn how to categorize, analyze, and even interpret the meanings underlying this material. Folklore informs us about our own identities, shedding light on who we are and how we think about the world around us.

The students in Forms of Folklore create their own folklore collections, and they use their newfound knowledge about classification to categorize the examples they collect. The youth visit the Folklore Archive on the Berkeley campus, where archivists introduce them to sample collections and discuss both form and content. Their instructor, whose area of specialization is the history and folklore of children's games around the world, guides his students through the process of gathering and studying lore, and along the way discloses why people spend their lives studying it.

In the Biotechnology class the instructor is an experienced high school teacher and also a liaison between the biotechnology industry and K–12 schools. She introduces youth to experiences that are not at all everyday ones for most of us. However, the experiences are matter-of-fact for groups of scientists on campus and around the world, some of whom the teacher knows well and to whom she introduces her students. One of the student activities involves preparing agarose gels for DNA electrophoresis, a technique for sorting DNA based on size. Subsequently, the students use this technique to solve problems akin to those being tackled in professional labs all over the Bay Area. The students also learn the process known as *PCT*, or *polymerase chain reaction*, which allows the students to churn enormous quantities of DNA from a single sample.

The Functional Neuroanatomy instructor is a doctoral student studying nerve regeneration in the elderly after strokes. In class the students work together on study guides as they prepare for their midterm and final examinations. These were among the questions on which they combined their considerable knowledge:

> If you raised your hand in class to answer a question, what brain areas might be involved? How does that information get to your arm?

> If you suddenly found yourself eating way too much but never feeling full, what part of your brain might not be working right?

> What part of the brain mediates the sneeze and vomit reflexes? Be as specific as possible. Why do you think it is important for our survival that we have these reflexes?

> When a police officer stops someone for probably drinking and driving, the officer has the driver do things like touching his/her nose with his/her eyes closed. Why is that? What part of the brain is probably most affected by alcohol?

> Explain why soap operas do not portray amnesia very accurately. In your answer include two major types of amnesia and discuss which is more common.

> Why is it *not* the case that memories are like snapshots or videos?

Students in the Architecture course routinely use some aspect of the campus as their vehicle into design. One year the Architecture students tested campus accessibility; they toured the campus in wheelchairs loaned by the campus Disabled Students Center. At one point they found themselves in a building that had designed an accessible entry but no accessible exit. That was a profound lesson for the students about the human aspects of architecture and about how much more there is to learn than meets an uninformed eye; and it provided a reminder for campus administrators as well.

YOUR IDEAS NOT ONLY COUNT, THEY INFORM OTHERS

Snapshots of the work the students do in a variety of courses are visible at the end-of-summer Poster Fair that a teacher initiated some years ago for classes interested in sharing the products of their time together. Of course the Poster Fair itself resembles experiences that graduate students and various academics and professionals are quite familiar with, from presenting at national conferences. At the annual ATDP Poster Fair for the summer of 2004, visitors listened to presentations from the Introduction to Engineering group on topics that included The Class A Headphone Driver, Truss Bridges, and the [History of] Motion Sensors. That same summer the Scientific Investigations class, a course for middle school students, shared posters on projects like these:

> Do video games increase your pulse rate?
> Proving Sir Isaac Newton's 1st law of motion
> Does temperature affect the rate of carbon dioxide given off by fermentation?
> What kind of soda will produce the most millevolts of electricity?

At the end of each summer the students in the Shakespeare as Theatre class present scenes to an audience of parents and peers in Faculty Glade. (One summer a scene had Juliet speaking from the branches of a tree; this took place only after the students gained permission for using the tree from university groundskeepers.) The culminating activity for the course titled Practice of Law takes place off campus. Students go to a San Francisco trial courtroom to conduct a mock trial in front of a very real practicing San Francisco judge, who evaluates their efforts.

WHO JOINS THE CLUB? WHO LIVES IN THE ATDP COMMUNITY?

Who are the students of ATDP and what exactly do they experience in their classes? Is the program the province of the rich, the White, the privileged few? Do the opportunities and experiences turn out to look more like "school" as most of us know it than we have suggested so far? And, most important, what do the students, the teachers, and their shared experiences tell us about engaging children and youth in serious conversations and study within and across the academic domains?

Who Gathered in Wheeler Hall That Saturday?

The students and families gathered in Wheeler Hall for the ATDP orientation came from some of the wealthiest communities in the San Francisco Bay Area: Tiburon, Pacific Heights, Orinda. And they came from some of the poorest communities in the San Francisco Bay Area: Bay View-Hunters Point, the Iron Triangle in Richmond, West Oakland. They came from rural communities: Coalinga, Huron, Avenal. They came from abroad, even from warring countries: Israel and Iraq. The students were sons and daughters of doctors, lawyers, astronomers, astrologists, acupuncturists, funeral home directors, housecleaners, lettuce pickers, newspaper editors, pistachio packers, restaurant cooks, celebrated chefs, spiritualists, teachers, vintners, veterinarians. A count revealed 52 different first languages represented among the student cohort.

Who Enrolled in Deena G.'s Class?

As an example, consider the 21 students (of 1,400 enrolled that summer in the Secondary Division) who selected Deena G.'s Intermediate Writing course from the ATDP program book. The students enrolled in the class were almost evenly divided between male (10) and female (11). They were spread by age from one student who had just completed 7th grade to two who had just completed 10th grade. The 21 students came to ATDP from 18 different schools. Consistent with the diversity of the San Francisco Bay Area, the languages other than English spoken in these students' homes included Cantonese, Mandarin, Korean, Spanish, Farsi, and German; five homes were monolingual English. Seven of the students had taken part in ATDP in previous summers; the rest were new to the program.

This diverse group of American youth would meet twice a week for 6 weeks on the Berkeley campus. They would read, write, and talk about writing (their own, their classmates', and the list of authors the teacher introduced them to, including bell hooks, Alice Walker, Andre Lorde, Oliver Sacks, Margaret Atwood, June Jordan, Amy Tan, Maxine Hong Kingston, Janice Mirikitani, Kit Yuen Quan, Cornelius Eady, Richard Wright, Carolyn Heilbrun, and Frank Chin). They would encounter a teacher who was passionate about writing and committed to welcoming youth into the academic conversation.

Why Do They Join?

Year after year they come because there is nothing easy about the program. They come because they know that the classes will expose them to ideas and people they might otherwise never meet. ATDP students are very clear on that point and comment frequently in their end-of-the-program evaluations that they greatly appreciate the self-respect they build, the new things they have to think about, and the many uses they find for their new knowledge and skills. When alumni/ae write or speak about the program, most frequently they single out as "most valuable to their educational lives" the diversity of others with whom they worked and had fun at ATDP.

A BRIEF HISTORY: FROM MINING TALENT TO GROWING IT

We write about the Academic Talent Development Program because it is unconventional, because the intense work is within reach of a wide range of students with a wide range of educational backgrounds. We write about it because it sees its purpose as the cultivating of academic talents and skills. We write about ATDP because it is connected to what people do in the real world, and because it shows its students the myriad ways in which they are connected to each other and to the world of ideas. It was not always so.

The program we are writing about began in 1981 as an offshoot of the Johns Hopkins Academic Talent Search Program and was called the UC Berkeley Gifted Program. For the first six years the program held a recruiting meeting—filling the grand 2,000-seat Zellerbach Hall—for students and parents of students in the sixth grade to tell them about the benefits of being identified as gifted and about the possibilities for participating in a highly selective summer opportunity.

Anyone interested in applying to the UC Berkeley Gifted Program was required to take the Scholastic Aptitude Test (SAT) from the Educational Testing Service (ETS) and have the scores sent directly to the Gifted Program. (The acronym SAT has remained the same over many years, but the letters now refer to the Scholastic Achievement Test.) Sixth-grade students who scored at or above the 50th percentile for college-going freshmen, on either the verbal or the quantitative portions of the test, were invited to join the program. Many were called, few were chosen. Students invited to take part based on their identification as gifted (using a norm-referenced test score as was common at the time) could select from among a small handful of courses. The program offered "individual appointments for psychoeducational evaluations" at an additional cost.

The program has changed significantly over the years; its brochure marks nicely some of the critical changes. For the summer of 1987, the 6th year of the program, the brochure still referred to the UC Berkeley Gifted Program. The following year the brochure continued with the name of UC Berkeley Gifted Program but added the subheading For Academic Talent Development. One year later, in the 8th year of the program, the brochure and all printed descriptions referred for the first time to the name still used today: UC Berkeley Academic Talent Development Program.

Even in 1989, although the name had changed, the guiding orientation was consistent with the program origins. According to the 1989 brochure, students still were expected to submit an SAT score as part of the application. The brochure indicates that "12, 13, and 14-year-old students are expected to rank at or above the 50th percentile for college-bound seniors on either the verbal or mathematics sections. Older students are expected to rank higher."

BECOMING ATDP

The changes that were taking place were not made lightly. The director was concerned about the exclusive nature of the program and wondered whether it could reasonably become more inclusive. A pilot program begun in the summer of 1987 included 16 students from the California Central Valley. These students did not have the educational background that in the past had been expected for ATDP, and yet they seemed to be proceeding quite well. A developmental psychologist was invited to create a year-long seminar for program personnel and interested teachers from feeder schools to study gifted and talented education and to think about new ways of identifying, selecting, and working with students who, under the older system, might not have appeared on the radar.

For the summer of 1990, the change in program orientation was complete. No longer was the program interested in a search for gifted students. Instead, the program had shifted its focus to academic talent and its development. The 1990 Academic Talent Development Program brochure makes no mention of the SAT in the information about admissions. In place of the previous admission discussion the brochure now noted:

> Students are invited to attend the program on the basis of performance on standardized achievement tests and evidence of creative

activities. In evaluating each application, the Program considers teacher nominations, student products (such as samples of creative writing, descriptions of science projects), and special interests. Official school designation of "gifted" is not required for admission to the program.

Making Informed Selections from Among More Choices

Also following the research on the development of talent and expertise, ATDP is self-conscious about its mechanisms for helping students adopt as their own and identify as a member of the academic community. The program aims to get students hooked on subject matter. Teachers encourage play with subject-specific knowledge and ideas. They aim to create a sense of wonder and intrigue. In the language of Whitehead (1929), and the Bloom (1985) studies on the development of talent in the arts, sports, and intellectual arenas, ATDP coursework encourages students to develop a romance with the subject.

The aim of inviting students into an academic community with significant standards and always in the process of renewing itself is a vision the program tries to convey from its first communications with students and their parents. It is a vision embedded in the program brochure, and then again in the orientation, and then again in the welcome letters the teachers write to their students, and then again in the first assignments. It is a vision the program hopes is embedded in the selection of students and teachers and in every meeting of every class.

The brochure for the program for the summer of 1990 also exploded in size. Many new courses were offered, and this was the first year that descriptions of each course, as prepared by the teacher, were included in the brochure with the application material. Before 1990, students and parents chose courses based on their title (Latin, Pascal, The Expository Essay, Algebra I, Astronomy, Marine Biology, and so on). Beginning in 1990, students and parents could read about each course, as you might in a college catalog, and could make course choices based on topics to be studied and the ways the teacher explained the instructional experience. Here are two examples of the course descriptions:

INTRODUCTION TO GREEK

Why study dead languages? They're not dead; they're only hibernating. In fact, the study of classical languages (Greek and Latin) is one of the most valuable studies a student can undertake. They teach discipline, vocabulary, and memorization skills which are of use in many academic pursuits; and most important, they offer a gateway to the culture of the people whose achievements form the basis of Western civilization. Besides, Homer and Herodotus are good reading, and they're better in the original language.

The Greek course will introduce students to reading and writing the Greek alphabet and to the beginnings of the grammar, syntax, and vocabulary of Classical Greek. In order to acquaint students with ancient Greek culture, mythology, and thought, we will read selections from Greek poetry, philosophy, drama, and history (such as Homer, Plato, Euripides, and Herodotus) in translation.

PALEONTOLOGY: IN SEARCH OF THE PAST

Explore the science of paleontology and learn how paleontologists recreate earth's past environments and life forms. Following a brief introductory section covering basic principles of paleontology and evolutionary theory, students will engage in a survey of the major events of earth-life history. Emphasis will be placed on such topics as the origin of life, life in ancient seas, colonization of the land, evolution of the dinosaurs, the first mammals, the age of mammals, and the search for human ancestors. Laboratory projects and field trips will familiarize students with techniques used by paleontologists in collecting, preparing, and analyzing different types of fossils.

This course is highly recommended as an entry-level science course.

DEVELOPMENT ISN'T ONLY FOR STUDENTS; IT'S FOR PROGRAMS, TOO

Today, the program looks much like its 1990 manifestation, only larger and further developed. Year after year the program has attracted more students. In the summer of 1992, for example, 762 students enrolled in the Secondary Division program. A decade later, in the summer of 2002, 1,426 students enrolled. The 2002 enrollment likely will remain the largest for the program. ATDP has been limited since then not by who might be interested or eligible, but, rather, by the number of classrooms on the Berkeley campus available to the program in any given summer.

The Elementary Division program, for students completing kindergarten through Grade 6 (see discussion in Chapter 3), similarly has drawn increasing numbers of students each year. In the summer of 1992, the Elementary Division enrollment was 581. Ten years later, in the summer of 2002, 1,006 students enrolled. Again, enrollment since then has been limited not by the number of qualified and interested students but by the number of classrooms in the elementary school near public transportation that houses the program.

ATDP IS NOT SMALL, BUT IT'S VERY PERSONAL

Although the current movement in education is in the direction of "small schools," the director of ATDP feels no need to limit the student population for the sake of keeping the program small. She is concerned that the "small schools" movement inadvertently ends up limiting the choices students might have in what to study, when to study something, and with whom to study. Since the ATDP aim is to offer serious academic and intellectual possibilities that youth might choose for themselves, and then to help students successfully negotiate their choices, the number of serious options available to students must be as large as possible.

Even with about 1,400 students in the Secondary Division, ATDP *is* a "small" program. It is small in two ways. First, ATDP is small in relation to the number of students who might be interested and might benefit from this academic opportunity. Second, ATDP is small in the sense underlying the "small schools" movement: it is personal, very personal.

The director works with just four full-time staff to serve all the students and their families. Every participating student is known to one or more of the staff. The staff treat the students as if they were part of their own families. At the June orientation in Wheeler Hall, a mother who described the welcoming (also noisy, cluttered, and crowded) ATDP office made that point with great humor to the gathered families, aiming to help the newcomers feel a little more comfortable with sending their children off to Berkeley.

ATDP is like a small town, with its large and well-lived-in office in Tolman Hall as the center of the town's action. Students and families routinely stop by to ask questions, share stories about the life in the program and outside of it, seek advice, and offer suggestions. ATDP reminds us not to confuse the *number* of students served with the *ways* those students are served—in this case with an emphasis on personal relationships. Undoubtedly this small-town feel contributes significantly to the long-term commitments students and families make to the program.

ATDP not only attracts students, it also has holding power. That is, students return, summer after summer. One of the students who spoke at the June orientation in Wheeler Hall was returning for his ninth summer.

He started with ATDP as a first grader, and told stories about the Greek Mythology he studied that summer. This summer he would enroll in Introduction to Psychology. (His mother joked that this isn't much of a movement—in 8 years, her son had moved only from "Psyche to psych." Interestingly, he is presently majoring in psychology in college.) Of course few students have had such extended experience with ATDP. But many do return for two or three or four or more summers.

Over the years the program has built loyal constituencies. Younger brothers and sisters followed in the steps of their older siblings. Students from schools in the area recruited others from those same schools. Students and parents raised money by selling cakes and cookies or—the Coalinga, Huron, and Avenal community's famous tradition—having a cowpie drop contest so that groups of boys and girls from their communities could attend. Yes, ATDP has a Web site that includes all details regarding the program and the process of applying to it (http://atdp.berkeley.edu). And ATDP does prepare and send thousands of copies of a program catalog to past participants, all schools in the area, and all others who request the information. But, in no small measure, word of mouth recruits students from year to year, and ATDP encourages students to invite their friends to apply.

In recent years, slightly more than half of the students each summer have been returning students. This number is even larger than it seems at first glance, because students "graduate" from ATDP after Grade 11 and each year new seventh graders enter. In the language of Silicon Valley, the program is "sticky."

THE GOOD NEWS IS THAT EVEN GOOD THINGS CHANGE AND EVOLVE

Both the growth in enrollment and the "stickiness" of the program have had their effect on the courses offered each summer. Over the years some courses have remained much the same; others have been added or dropped. Changes sometimes have been the result of who was available to teach, and what each teacher thought was most worth students' time and effort. Some changes have been the result of deliberations about enrichment versus acceleration. Although the program does offer classes that allow students to advance further or more quickly in high school, those are not the rule.

As the catalog indicates, "It is the Program's intention to augment and enrich the schooling experience, not to replace or supplant what is offered in a student's regular school." Some changes have been the result of conversations with students and parents that led to new courses and to new sequences of courses for students who were interested in deeper studies following a first or second experience. Class activities for specific courses change regularly, as "sticky" classes evolve.

ESPECIALLY "STICKY," VIRTUALLY SPEAKING

For well over a decade, The Internet Classroom (TIC) has brought together the largest and perhaps the most diverse groups of students and has, through the wonders of technology, brought together students from very low income communities to the wealthiest communities in the area, and these students have formed communities uniquely their own. The depth and duration of friendships made through TIC are remarkable. The class and its many students—some years, upwards of 70 students—have also brought to ATDP at large various teaching uses of technology. In thinking about TIC, Lloyd Nebres, creator of TIC and the ATDP database as well as a core ATDP staffer for over 20 years, says that he sees TIC operating exactly as ATDP does. Or is it vice versa? Here, Nebres tells the TIC story himself:

> ATDP's class, The Internet Classroom, began as a course on Web design and HTML. I started TIC, as it came to be known, in the mid-1990s, the halcyon years of the Internet and World Wide Web explosion; predictably, ATDP students applied to take it in droves. From the start, I wanted to encourage and mentor students as creative, thinking individuals and artists. I wanted to mentor them as writers, yes, but in other creative domains also—photography, music, and, indeed, as visionaries of Web design user interfaces. That last domain encompassed cutting-edge developments, as adults in tech startups in the wider world were at that moment creating those very interfaces for the rapidly evolving Internet. My not-so-hidden agenda trumped the merely technological aspect of TIC, as students in my summer classes engaged in critical thinking and analytical writing—skills they could put to good use in as many other subjects and fields they would encounter in their regular schooling.
>
> The class has lots and lots of thinking and writing in it in the form of narrative responses to a daily journal question that asks students to reflect on issues concerning the Internet and society, and on technology in general. By the summer of 2000, we no longer did this by e-mail. We incorporated Weblog writing as an essential

practice, long before so-called blogs became popular. Weblogging their journals meant that students were now writing for an audience—not just in our classes, but for a potentially much larger one in the broader Internet itself. [Please note that until they graduate from high school, members of our online community are monitored in their ATDP-sponsored Internet communications. Even the most academically able youth need to be protected by adults. NHG]

Quickly, a fascinating—and mostly unintended—consequence arose. Beyond each summer session, TIC students continued engaging with each other simply as far-flung new friends hailing from many different school districts in the San Francisco Bay Area and beyond the state and country. After meeting and getting to know each other over the summer, it was only natural that they would keep and nurture these new friendships, and also natural to engage in it online. Many such friendships would turn out to be strong, intense ones; while centered around our "technological personae" as members of the TIC community, these friendships were also typical ones that any kids develop as they grow through their teenage years. And—gulp—some of the students from the early TIC groups are now also discussing online their careers, marriages, and the arrival of offspring.

So, online community building became an intrinsic part of the class; not just a classroom without walls, but one not bounded by time either. When the students discovered that they could learn a lot about cutting edge Web technology and the Internet from one another's independent investigations and common experiences, a natural and long-lasting basis for forging bonds across the widest range of ATDP students formed. Instead of the academic one-upmanship common in secondary schools, in the TIC community knowledge sharing was an inherent quality, perhaps the most valued one. The virtues of peer review were also developed over time, as students' Web site design work and writings became lucid expressions of nascent but coherent world views, vetted as it were by the opinions and feedback of their peers.

The TIC community has evolved to encompass the ATDP's community at large. A new entity called The Virtual ATDP (TVA) attempts to replicate in broader fashion what TIC wrought in its small Web-design-based community. TVA has the same ethos as TIC as a place online where ATDP students, mentors, teachers, and staff can thrive, virtually and in 3-space. TIC itself is now taught by former students: Nikki Sung, a doctoral student of computer science, and Vic Taylor, who also teaches "computers" during the year. Other former TIC students are teachers in other ATDP classes, such as Java, Programming in C++, and Robotics. Still other former TIC students now work in many other classrooms creating online records of class happenings and providing for each participating class the same encouragement of ongoing conversations among students and teachers about immediate course topics, about current research, and possibilities for the future—near and distant.

Lloyd Nebres, just as he said he would, told the story of ATDP's Secondary Division as he told the story of The Internet Classroom. While his story tells a great deal about the program, it represents only a part (albeit a big part) of the story we have to tell. Please recall what Whitehead said about "romantic engagement" with learning, what Duckworth said about "having wonderful ideas," and then add lots of giggling and running around. Now you have a good introduction to Chapter 3, which puts on display not only ATDP's Elementary Division but also how all of these things fit together and how they all lead to membership in the academic club.

When Learning Is Child's Play

AFTER FOUR YEARS OF OPERATION, the Academic Talent Development Program (then named the Gifted Program) expanded its focus to include younger girls and boys. The goal, as with the older students, was to offer them opportunities that they might not have in their home schools, chances to see for themselves what it is like to seize learning as something they could opt to pursue in the company of like-minded children. With that as the objective, albeit within a conventional frame of reference, in 1985 the Elementary Division began as the Young Scholars Program, aiming to serve already-identified gifted students in Grades 3 to 5 through cross-age, interdisciplinary classes. While such young children would not yet have been presented on the stage at Zellerbach Auditorium as having been found via a search for talent, they had all been identified as gifted by their own school. Originally, the expectation was that children coming to the program were able to excel in serious study by using knowledge and skills they already possessed.

As the program began to evolve toward its present purpose and shape, ATDP came to view and work with its students, through play, through romantic engagement, to enter the academic community. Engle (2005) describes the goal and context perfectly:

> One important change in how we view children is that we now see them as budding experts who absorb information and ideas from experts within their culture, and who practice, amassing strategies, information, and techniques that lift their thinking to a higher level within that domain or discipline. Their knowledge therefore is both culturally specific and domain specific. Children's skills emerge from experience with a certain set of materials and goals and reflect the community and habits within which they are learned and used. (p. 171)

WHILE FIGURING THINGS OUT, CHANGES BEGIN

In spring 1987, as ATDP Secondary Division (still the Gifted Program) began transforming itself, so did the Young Scholars Program. The ATDP staff worked to develop a setting where elementary-school-aged students would delve deeply into disciplines that they might not yet know existed. The program for elementary-school-aged children would need to provide an opportunity for ATDP to invite into the academic community young children who would discover that they are scholars, especially students who had previously been absent from any roll call of the gifted and had been mostly invisible in searches for talent.

Unlike the present ATDP Elementary Division, the Young Scholars Program was freestanding and did not aim to articulate with the program for secondary school students. However, within a couple of years, the original program for students in Grades 3 to 5 expanded to include children who had completed kindergarten through Grade 2. Inadvertently or deliberately, the decision to add the two lower grades marked the beginning of a departure from requiring that students be identified as gifted by their own schools. These children were too young for that.

As they had done previously, students completing Grade 6 attended the UC Berkeley campus-based secondary school program. This configuration reflected more an intention to add younger students to the existing program than to make the program congruent with the program for older students that was held on the Berkeley campus.

However, absent a grounded notion of how children proceed from kindergarten through Grade 12, the best ATDP could offer would be two freestanding programs. Even if the programs each provided fine experiences, they would remain devoid of experiences that guide students through complex developmental transitions. That limitation had to be addressed if ATDP was to meet the academic and social needs of its students as they matured.

It was while ATDP staff were learning to create an inclusive, developmentally based selection process that they began to think systematically about the requirements for an articulated program. Using a developmental lens, it became clear that sixth graders would be better served in the elementary school program than on the Berkeley campus. In order to create an optimal fit, however, ATDP would need to create an "in-between" experience for sixth graders—one that provided the social support of the elementary school program but also had increased opportunities for independent learning inside and outside of class. In other words, sixth graders needed a transitional program.

Before and during the building of an articulated program that included these opportunities for transition, the K–5 program lived in the shadow of the UC Berkeley campus-based division. Over time, ATDP's participating families have seen the programs grow to equal import in the eyes of outside watchers as well as ATDP insiders. But at the start, the family orientations for both the K–5 and 6–11 divisions were held in the same place, the huge Pauley Ballroom on the Berkeley campus.

FINDING A HOME AND CONSOLIDATING LESSONS LEARNED

The Young Scholars Program/Elementary Division experienced difficulty finding a home at an elementary school and had to move several times. It was evicted by one school district, and then had to move three more times because of construction. This created logistical nightmares for loyal families: They didn't know where they might be taking their children next. Now, however, the quality of ATDP life at its present home is outstanding. The site is beautiful and the school is situated near the hub of several freeways that easily bring both wealthy and very low income families to the school. Mass transit use is facilitated by a school bus to bring children from the BART station 2 miles away.

The move to its current site marked the first time ATDP had been invited by a school principal and deputy superintendent to house itself at a school site; before that, a lot of begging had to be done. This school district's chief academic officer, Dr. Kaye E. Burnside, then a site principal, had taken on the task of revitalizing a school slated for closure. Burnside had made the school's motto "a private school education at public school prices," which some took to be an irony. The school's urban, low-performing, district was then in bankruptcy and many, if not most, middle-class families had fled. Burnside, however, saw it differently. She pictured her students and others from similar schools as being well served by ATDP if ATDP were a convenient presence in their neighborhood, and she saw her school and ATDP both benefiting from a close collaboration.

This collaboration with an urban school district has advanced ATDP's evolution toward creating an elementary school program that can be replicated and viable within other urban school districts, in all classes, for all children.

In addition, having a functioning connection to public elementary schools has permitted ATDP to be part of a vital learning cycle. Collaboration with an urban school district has given ATDP opportunities to test and verify research, to have its process and procedures tested for generalizability, and thereby refined. But more on that later. For now, let us proceed to ATDP's home at Washington Elementary School in Richmond, California.

INVITING YOUNG STUDENTS
INTO THE ACADEMIC COMMUNITY

The school's auditorium provided much more appropriate surroundings for orientations for young children than did the Berkeley campus. Here, families, large and small, pour into the elementary school's multipurpose room. Since school auditoriums are smaller than university ballrooms designed to hold 1,000 people or more, and since the program enrollment is very large, the orientation is held in four packed sessions. Just as at the Secondary Division orientation, people who haven't seen each other since the summer before embrace and take the seats they've saved for one another.

New families, startled by the hubbub, are quickly taken under the wing of an ATDP staff member or brave the crowd and settle in, their children usually finding someone of their own size to sit with. Some other new students sit for a while snuggled onto their parent's lap, unsure of what to make of the whole thing. The four sessions divide the audience by grades, so that presentations can address separately the concerns and questions of primary school students from those of students ready to enter seventh grade.

In each session returning students chatter excitedly, anticipating the start of a favorite class many picked out during the program's open house the previous summer. The excitement runs especially high around the topic of meeting their teacher; in the eyes of the students their teachers are the stars of the elementary school program. On this Saturday, after the orientation meeting for kindergartners to third graders who would be attending class in the morning sections (most classes have a morning and an afternoon section so that more students might be served), students and families left the multipurpose room to find their own classroom and teacher.

Quite a number of the returning students present at K–3 orientation made themselves student hosts for the morning. These students were eager to show interested families around the school grounds, tell them all about the class(es) they had taken and the class they were going to take now, and most important, include a brief treatise on selecting from the ice cream choices available at recess. All made it clear that they were ready to supply additional advice if asked. Even returning first graders showed others that they are knowledgeable about the program, that the program belongs to them and that they are eager to invite others to join in the fun. They are confident that they know what needs to be done, and they want to teach what they know to others.

What Are the Course Choices? For Whom?

The Elementary Division's course offerings are organized by grade and offer course choices in humanities, mathematics, and the natural sciences. For kindergarten, the only two choices are both natural sciences, Rocky Reefs and Tide Pools and Oviparous Animals, but provide many opportunities to write and calculate as well. For other grades, choices include Greek Mythology for first graders; Writing and Drawing the World for second graders; Human Anatomy for third graders; Those Wonderful Simple Machines as well as Land of the Pharaohs for fourth graders, Lab Chemistry as well as Patterns and Functions in Math for fifth graders, Electron Madness for sixth graders, and many more that differ across the grades.

All classes are rich in content and filled with opportunities for engagement and fascination. And all classes invite young students to don the mantle of an academician in order to experience deep learning, deep knowledge, from inside the academic club. Later, we will provide detailed descriptions of a few of these exciting courses.

Induction into the Academic Club

In 1988 Kulani Marshall, a young woman who years later would teach an ATDP entomology course titled Bugs, Bugs, Bugs to second graders, was herself a kindergarten student at ATDP. She had thrown herself headlong into her first more-playful-than-formal introduction to laboratory science, studying Rocky Reefs and Tidepools. As do all serious scientists, she maintained a detailed lab journal. During the 2nd week of class, when the program director came to visit her class, young Kulani charged at breakneck speed to hand her open notebook to the director, "Nina, Nina, can you read this to me? It's my lab journal." The director answered, "Kulani, this looks very important. Why don't you read it to me?" Kulani replied, "I can't. I don't know how to read yet."

Kulani had been inducted into the academic club; she was doing what scientists do, in all the ways that they are done by students with a passion for science. And she was doing all these things in the best of modes. She was role-taking; she was playing within the structure of a classroom that provided many rich opportunities for anticipatory socialization. Eighteen years later, with her course Bugs! Bugs! Bugs! Kulani extended a similar invitation to children, encouraging them to acquire knowledge through direct and indirect learning about new roles they have yet to assume. Kulani's invitation states:

> We will both observe and explore firsthand the life cycles of various insects. Together we will use the scientific method while recording our observations, creating artful models, and examining the habitats. A highlight of the course will be our insect collections, which we will organize and label. Come join us as we research and celebrate their growth and transformation!

PLAY: THE BEST WAY TO ACCRUE INTELLECTUAL CAPITAL

In myriad ways ATDP invites young students into the academic conversation—the authentic one that takes place when people who know a lot get together to discuss the topics about which they're most passionate. The heart of the conversation takes place between ATDP teachers and students in their classrooms. The conversations don't end there, however. They can be heard continuing on the playground, in car pools, at home, and at regular school the following fall.

When parents visit Nora Trustman's room to inquire about her popular Greek Mythology class for first graders, she recommends that children learn mythology as "a nice springboard for when they start writing stories on their own." She uses the tale of Pandora's Box as an example of children learning the story, itself very rich in visual details, and then adapting the format to a story of their own telling. First, students learn, perform, and discuss the myth. Then they construct a Pandora's Box of their own, filling it with significant objects to tell parents, guests, and fellow students a fascinating story of their own.

For the parents' reference during the course, and for students' reference long after the summer ends, Nora Trustman has created a bound handbook with a bibliography. The handbook is filled with activities for children and parents to do together during the course of the class. The syllabus contains a shortened version of each of the myths to be studied in class, to be read in pace with the class, but not ahead, so as to maintain surprise and magic. There is a pronunciation guide, word lists, and additional resources. There is also an open invitation to students and parents to share books and ideas as they discover them.

Trustman's book also contains this request to families:

> Homework is assigned twice a week. It is designed to enrich and refresh the student's memory of the day's work. A Think-Write-Draw journal format allows students to respond [using different modes]. . . . Responses may be dictated and transcribed by a parent or older sibling. However, we would like to see original student work.

As an aside, we should note that there is plenty of additional homework support in the classroom for two groups of children—those whose family is unable to provide assistance and guidance, and those whose family provides too much assistance and guidance. In this way, all students have the opportunity to show their original work in the way that they wish it to be presented.

By the time her students have prepared for the Mount Olympus feast, held on the last day of class, they have steeped themselves in the tradition of Greek myths and each student has become a resident expert on the god or goddess each has selected to portray. All know so many specifics of many kinds of stories that they are able to allude to and apply lessons from mythology to their own unique and shared experiences.

However, when inviting students to join her on Mount Olympus, Ms. Trustman uses different language, promising that "we will meet the heroes, tricksters, monsters, gods, and goddesses of Ancient Greece. We will dress as [our] favorite mythical figure, entertain guests with role plays of myths we have studied, and we will all feast on the delights of the gods and goddesses of Mount Olympus."

The interaction of imagination, play, and mythological characters ripe for role-play provides a magical framework within a context perfect for absorbing huge amounts of information. Each 3½-hour class meeting is replete with movement, action, color, art, and music, all centered on excitement made possible by possessing more and more detailed knowledge of Greek mythology. Just as in the relationship of children and dinosaurs and museums of natural history, the more complex or obscure the various stories are, the more likely that children are to see them as providing the greatest value to the romance of their play and engagement with the subject. Here, students bring specialized vocabulary and esoteric information into the conversation reinforced and extended by the group.

Again, Fun for All and Far More Significant for Some

Experiences from their mythology classroom provide students with ready allusions commonly used in literature and with a greater facility with language. This is terrific fun for children whose conversation with parents and significant adults already encourages such speech and such play. But consider the contribution this kind of learning makes to the academic lives of children with less out-of-school exposure to the ideas and references in which much of their future study has its roots.

The invitation to join the academic conversation is made more practical and authentic as it arms all students with prior knowledge and important learning experiences, all built through play. Consider also how much more likely students are to view the serious study of literature and writing if they have already developed rich, knowledge-filled experiences with allusion and metaphor. All that abstract stuff harkens back to favorite memories of exciting play and complex stories that they themselves have created and told.

Be Sure to Encrust Your Chariot with Many Jewels!

One of the best parts of the director's job is the opportunity to participate in classroom activities in all classes. On one particular morning, as she entered the mythology class, met by trays upon trays of sparkling "jewels" of every imaginable color and size, the director heard this admonition being made by the teacher, "Remember, girls and boys, these are golden chariots of the gods. So, encrust them with jewels selected to please the deity for whom you're building it."

As Ms. Trustman turned around, she gave the students a knowing look, "Did I tell you that as soon as we started to decorate our chariots, Nina would show up? I think that decorating the chariots in here must be her favorite part of the whole program." Indeed, as a metaphor for the kind of learning that goes on at Elementary Division, that is certainly true. Of course, as an opportunity to encrust golden cardboard chariots with as many jewels as she wants, it's true too.

We do want to assure you that the timing of this visit to the mythology class was entirely coincidental. Besides, it's only one of the director's favorite parts of Elementary Division. Other favorites are plastic soda bottles going off like rockets, concrete boats floating (or sinking), coffee-filter kidneys filtering ketchup, children writing poems in the sand at the bay's shore, students explaining their Rube Goldberg inventions, kindergartners identifying creatures in tidepools, and third graders horrifying their parents as they weigh out the grams of fat in fast foods.

Please Take More, Please Ask More Questions, Please Laugh

One Friday, during the 90 minutes of class time after recess, students continued their examination of mythological creatures, with the Minotaur being the main topic of the afternoon. The first graders had heard, and some had read on their own, descriptions of Minotaur and stories of how he came to be confined within a labyrinth made so intricate, so complex, that escape from it should be impossible. The students giggled or shrieked with varying degrees of ghoulish delight or horror as they discussed the every-seventh-year feeding of seven Athenian boys to the Minotaur.

For homework the previous evening students had drawn Minotaur and written a brief essay about him: "Three or four sentences; not fewer—feel free to do more." Today, students were creating a mythological creature of their own. "Draw a new mythical creature. Remember, you can make up anything, because they're all imaginary. Be prepared to tell us what the creature eats, where it lives, what its habits are, and what it does all day."

Some tales were dear and sweet, some were heavy on detail and short on plot, some aimed to horrify the audience with hair-raising events intended to outdo anything heard to date. Everyone was supportive of everyone else's efforts, and materials needed to create each creature were gladly shared: "DeAysia, I think that this is what you're looking for for the front of your creature's head." "Does anyone have blue stars?" "Do you think that this green is really gross? I want a really, really gross color for my creature."

Oh, and Please Look Twice Before You Leap

As a summative activity for the day, the students were called together to view a 7-minute film about Theseus, the Athenian warrior-hero who slew the Minotaur, thus saving future Athenian children from being fed to the creature. Seated in a half-circle, students summarized what they already knew about the story and were eager to see its animated rendition. The group paid close attention, interjecting a few comments during especially exciting moments.

The tale came too quickly to its tragic conclusion: Theseus triumphantly sails back to Athens to his waiting father King Aegis, bringing with him his lady love, but forgetting to hoist the white sail selected to signal his father the news of his safe return and success of his mission. Instead, Theseus has forgotten to do as he had promised and has left the black sail unfurled, thus wrongly announcing his death to his loving father. Aegis' heart immediately breaks at the sight of the black sail, which he believes indicates that his son is dead, and Aegis throws himself off the cliffs into the sea that is now named in his honor, the Aegean Sea.

As the floor opened for discussion, a grinning Sean observed, "Maybe they should have taught King Aegis to look twice, and not just once, before he leaps." Students and adults alike were caught off guard by this display of spontaneous wit—such belly laughs are an excellent way to conclude a productive, knowledge-rich week.

Leaving for the weekend, students chatted excitedly and announced that they couldn't wait until Monday, when they would begin preparations for their expert presentations of the character they selected to become for the eagerly awaited Open House. Some left the classroom already having assumed their character's bearing and speaking in their character's voice.

Too Much Is Often Just Right for Curious Children

Just as in Rhona Weinstein's (2002) description of Landmark School, ATDP's parents also frequently "complain with humor" that their children are never ready to go home (Weinstein, p. 274). Making reference to her kinder-gartner's experience in a course titled Oviparous Animals, an ATDP par-ent "complained," "If I have to run to the dictionary one more time to learn words that my son uses when he tells me about his day, I'm going to scream. I feel like I have to have a dictionary with me every time I ask him what happened in class."

It was during one of these joking conversations that Sean's parents expressed their gratitude to the mythology teacher for providing the first classroom environment in which their son felt welcomed by his teacher and classmates. This was the first time he did not feel shunned for always hav-ing "a million questions."

At his highly academic (read: very expensive) private primary school, during his time in kindergarten and first grade, Sean's parents said that their son, almost daily, would come home crestfallen because he had been chided for "bothering" his teacher with too many questions that were "be-yond the scope of the class." His parents, on successive attempts to seek help from the school to keep alive their son's passion for learning, were repeatedly thwarted by the teacher and principal. Over and over, they had been told that there is an extensive curriculum to be gotten through, thus little time is left for extraneous, off-track, questions. By the end of first grade, Sean had already asked his parents if it's a bad thing to be smart, and had expressed his worries that he'd never have friends at school.

After the school year ended, Sean joined the Greek Mythology class and was astounded to find a room filled with children just like him. They shared his passion for questioning, for wanting to know why; they under-stood his jokes, and they enjoyed it when he laughed at theirs. Happily, few of the children present came from schools and classrooms similar to Sean's. But for those who did, instead of feeling chastised for wanting to know more, here they joined all of the children in pursuing their interests even farther than they knew they could go.

All thrive in an environment where questions are met with recommen-dations for how and where to pursue the knowledge sought. All thrive in an environment where they are challenged, encouraged, and supported as they take intellectual risks in pursuit of new ideas.

We know of at least four ATDP alumni who began a conversation in Nora Trustman's first-grade mythology class that set their imaginations so on fire that by Grade 12 they still had so many unanswered questions about the myths and the classics that they decided to pursue even further study in college. One of the four recently completed her doctoral studies in classics. Their mythology class had made explicit the possibilities cre-ated through classical studies, a field into which they had been warmly invited and actively inducted into its community of scholars. They had tried on the pursuit, tried on the roles of scholars, and played with mythological characters and their exciting stories. They found that if they wanted to know more and more, they would need to explore their increasingly refined questions in ever-greater depth, something they were well prepared to do. They also learned the importance of "not knowing" and the vital contributions to knowledge made my asking, questioning, seeking, trying, and trying again.

The point here, of course, is not that the first-grade mythology class is intended to create and mold classics scholars. ATDP's goal is for children to develop their own interests and inclinations, to acquire new ways of learning, and new orientations—all aimed toward making new connections, building knowledge bases, and applying them to the greater world beyond the classroom.

Developing a Need to Know: Interests and Inclinations

During the 2005 orientation to Force and Motion, a physics class for fourth graders, instructors Ella Stein and Edd Cooper introduced their course by extending an irresistible invitation into the serious study of physics. It is irresistible because it promises that "We will spend 3 weeks of balls falling and things flying. We will build a hovercraft on which you and your parents will ride at the ATDP Open House." From the laughter, it was clear that students were gleefully picturing how their parents might look zipping slightly above the playground's surface on a hovercraft they had built. At the same time some parents' laughter had a nervous tinge as they envisioned the same sight.

Every student in the group had a strong reason for being there—to have exciting, even thrilling, experiences with falling balls and flying parents. Who could resist an opportunity to become a serious student of physics with an invitation like that? So, when the "serious physics" is introduced, the reasons for its purposeful study are already well established. This is stuff you need to be able to know regarding falling balls and flying parents. Stein continued the introduction:

> We will start with gravity and friction, because these two mess up
> everything we do. As we proceed after that, we're dealing with
> Newton . . . each of his three laws. This will require us to work with
> lots of rolling objects and lots of flying objects. We hope that as you
> walk home from class each day you will look at things in a new and
> different way. For instance, each time you see a swing set, from
> now on, you'll see not only that it's fun but you'll understand what
> make the fun possible.

The class proceeded as introduced, the fun and excitement were as promised. At the conclusion of the class, Ella and Edd summed up student-selected highlights of the course. These included the effects of constant acceleration, which culminated with students shooting marshmallows from paper blowguns, then explaining the outcomes; the popular study of friction, which included constructing and riding on a simple hovercraft; using rolling and flying marbles when conducting experiments with motion; as well as studying Newton's third law by building and launching jet cars powered by baking soda and vinegar.

Again, here the teaching and learning are purposeful, intense, and intensely social. All are focused on problem solving in a collaborative manner and all learn that collaboration is a reciprocal process. For example, instructions for construction of the hovercrafts require that holes be drilled into two pieces of wood. As the two holes had to accommodate a through-bolt, Edd stressed how vital it is that the two holes line up and acknowledged that he knew how difficult the task of lining up the holes is, showing several of his own misaligned efforts. Very politely and timidly, a student said, "Edd, you know that it's only difficult if you drill the holes separately and then try to line them up. If you put the two pieces of wood on top of each other, hold them with a couple of big rubber bands, then drill, it's already lined up and you don't have any problems." The student had an advantage—his dad works for a framing contractor.

EVOKING CURIOSITY, INSPIRING PERSISTENCE

We aren't original in our notion of play, and we've already mentioned how the virtue of dreams and play have been extolled by philosophers including Alfred North Whitehead (1929) and Eleanor Duckworth (1987), and we have learned from Erving Goffman (1959, 1961) and others how anticipatory socialization permits students to become prepared for roles they might assume in the future. As much attention as we've brought to such learning, the topic deserves even more.

During a casual discussion with a small group of Elementary Division parents about Benjamin Bloom's and Lauren Sosniak's research into the development of world-class talent, a parent brought up the *Mr. Tompkins* books by physicist George Gamow as an example of romantic engagement that leads to serious study. These books tell amusing stories, with the principles of physics taken from Gamow's own lectures presented at the back of each of the books and linked point by point to the stories. The books are ones that physicists often recommend to people who want to learn about physics.

Playful Tales to Teach Serious Subject Matter

Mr. Tompkins in Wonderland (Gamow, 1940/2002), for example, tells playful tales that feature the timid but inquisitive bank clerk C. G. H. Tompkins, who takes a train trip that approaches the speed of light. The train's speed results in such uncommon effects as "relativity whiskers" and the shifting of light to the red and blue ends of the spectrum. As Mr. Tompkins sees the shifts and whiskers, the stories explain the strange effects of Einstein's special theory of relativity. George Gamow showed us marvelous applications of notions of play and imagination to the teaching of very serious physics, which in those many years before Stephen Hawking were cutting edge. Gamow encourages us to play with huge and hugely abstract ideas.

Many scientists, some of them parents of current ATDP students and some more famous people like Nobel Laureates Francis Crick and Robert Wilson, have cited the Tompkins series as having stimulated their youthful fascination with science. Gamow himself traced his own love of science to youthful play, for example, having been captivated by astronomy after his father gave him a small telescope to play with for his 13th birthday (Harper, 2000, p. 14).

Learning to Ask Why on a Stupendous Scale

ATDP parent Achilles Speliotopous, a physicist, observed:

> If I had known about the books when I was a kid, I would have been drawn to them first because they would have fed my need to know, and then through their various descriptions of what we knew about the world, they would have inspired me. Gamow put the ordinary—a bank clerk going on a train ride—into extraordinary conditions. That was how he described a world that we can all relate to, but then he asked, "What would happen if." This "what if" approach is what I use to understand things, to understand the importance of various parts of a complex whole. It is about seeking to answer why on a stupendous scale. I suspect that that is why so many students in the ATDP program are drawn to it as well. It's perfect teaching.

And it's perfect learning, too.

That's pretty heady stuff we're talking about, whether we are talking about Newton's laws in the Force and Motion class or here about special laws of relativity. Who can avail themselves of such specialized knowledge as fourth graders? If it is only children of scientists, or children of university graduates, or only children of well-to-do families, then that "perfect teaching" strategy would not be resulting in ideal learning. What then is happening in terms of children for whom science or mythology are not dinner table conversation? Who, for example, does select physics as a fourth grader?

Who Asks These Big Physics Questions at ATDP?

In 2005 there were 53 students enrolled in the two sections of Force and Motion, with all 106 parents reporting their own level of schooling and all 53 families reporting total family income. Fifteen families reported incomes at or below the poverty line, which qualified them for a full-tuition stipend, and 25 families reported an income of over $100,000 per year. Forty-one of the families speak English at home, and 12 speak a different language.

Thirty parents reported their level of schooling as being between grade school and 12 years (1 parent reported less than elementary school, 2 reported grade school through Grade 6, 8 reported some high school, and 19 reported high school or equivalent). The same number, 30 parents, reported a graduate or professional degree. The rest reported schooling—trade school or college—beyond high school through a bachelor's degree. What makes these data important to us is that at the end of the course, when ATDP students rate their learning experience, no student rated the class as being "too hard," and on a 4-point scale "amount learned" scored 3.86.

These data along with similar information over time from other classes affirm our understanding that children from all socioeconomic groups can and do learn together, and learn well. They learn more than three laws of physics, they learn more than literary allusions. They learn how to identify their intellectual peers, other children "just like them." And, as we showed in our discussions of Secondary Division students, "just like them" soon develops into "just like me."

ELEMENTARY AND SECONDARY DIVISIONS: TWO APPROACHES TOWARD ONE GOAL

Both ATDP divisions focus on purpose in the curricular and instructional choices teachers make; the same goes for the director's rubric in selecting new or replacement courses. Everything starts somewhere and moves students to someplace higher in skill level and deeper in knowledge and understanding. Toward this end, both divisions' class assignments aim to insure against cliques or other forms of social stratification being brought with students to ATDP class from students' home schools. Consequently, students from the same schools are distributed across different sections of a course. Things proceed differently when all must make new acquaintances in order to participate fully in the class. All are or become secure in the knowledge that anything that they do not already know can be learned and will be taught.

There are also significant differences between the two ATDP divisions, some of which were distinctions understood and accommodated from the beginning. Others surfaced and were addressed as the program became more developmental in its structure and philosophy.

Considerations in Course Placement:
By Age? By Grade? By Level of Preparation?

Student course placements in Elementary Division were originally based on the age of the child and were more broadly grouped (originally 2 to 3 years in an age range) than they are now. Over a short time, it became evident that there are levels of social learning reached through social experiences at various grade levels, so ATDP staff decided to group students by grade in school completed rather than by age. At the same time, the staff acknowledged that exceptions need to be made and that flexibility must be built in to assure minimum disruption or discomfort when exceptions are made. The expansive nature of ATDP course curricula and the open-ended nature of questions and activities mean that exceptions remain just that, exceptions.

For example, the sixth-grade transitional mathematics course, Baker Street Irregulars, prepares students to enter Secondary Division the following year by modeling independent work and scholarly work habits, including homework, yet it provides still-appreciated structures for imaginary play. In this case, the play points out clear uses for mathematical skills, like solving mysteries:

> When Sherlock Holmes had trouble with a mystery, he often turned to the Baker Street Irregulars, a group of London kids, to help him solve the problem. Like the Baker Street Irregulars, students in this class will be challenged by a series of unique problems. Since each problem is different, we will learn general problem-solving strategies that can be applied to a wide variety of problems—such as looking for patterns, drawing diagrams, working backward, questioning assumptions, and using logical reasoning—rather than specific procedures or formulas. We will work collaboratively and independently to solve a variety of problems ranging from realistic to fanciful, including picture problems, word puzzles, mysteries,

geometric problems, secret codes, logic problems, and strategy games. Students should expect 1–2 hours of homework per class. Each weekday assignment consists of six problems that make use of the techniques presented in class, and the weekend assignments involve extra creativity.

All students who have completed seventh grade enter Secondary Division, where ATDP offers an enrichment course for students who have not yet taken high school algebra and for whom an accelerated yearlong sequence taught in 18 class meetings is not desirable. The course, Foundations of Algebra, for seventh and eighth graders, offers less formal, more exploratory, experiences of the sort on which Baker Street Irregulars focuses. But the language of the subject matter and the organization of the learning experience are considerably more directed toward the introduction of big ideas, concepts, and skills for students to apply to the learning of algebra. The course Foundations of Algebra is described this way:

> Algebra is the language of mathematics and serves as a foundation for much of science and higher mathematics. In this course, we will focus on two topics at the heart of algebra—functions and abstraction. The theme of functions is a powerful and unifying concept, but difficult for many students to understand. The class will approach abstraction through mathematical problem solving by using algebra to generalize and extend our discoveries. Throughout the course, students will focus on developing deep understandings and connections between mathematical ideas, and on methods for exploring new mathematical situations (e.g., How do you know when you've solved a problem? How do you generalize from specifics?). *Homework per class meeting*: 3–4 hours

Exceptions? Except When?

Two months before Elementary Division applications were due, a parent, whose older daughter is now a 3rd-year university biology student, wrote to the director:

> Now it is time for us to focus our energies onto our younger one, Tanya. She has been in the ATDP elementary division for the last two years, and took writing courses, which she enjoyed, but on which we had insisted. However this year we want to accede to our daughter's wishes to move ahead in mathematics. While she is a fifth grader, we would like to talk with you about the possibility of

[our] signing her up for the Foundations of Algebra class in Secondary Division. Tanya is in advanced math in her class, and studies math on her own, with my wife's and my supervision. She has learned: positive and negative numbers, [solving] simultaneous linear equations in two to four variables, transform[ing] equations, inequalities, functions and graphs, square roots and quadratic equations. Right now, she is specifically eager to learn anything related to Pythagorean theorem. Reading the course description of Foundations of Algebra, it seems that Tanya has done quite a few things that are part of course. Therefore, we believe that she is ready and will do well. However, your opinion is critical for us. Therefore, please let me know what you consider could be the next step. If you have time, we want to come and discuss this with you in person and bring some of her work to show you. Your advice in this matter will be greatly appreciated. Looking forward to hearing from you, I remain with my best regards,
    Rahim

Even with her stellar qualifications, it was still important to have a serious discussion with Tanya. The final decision to accelerate her entry to Secondary Division would need to rest with her. She needed to consider the ways that she would be constrained by the move, in addition to the opportunities she would have to pursue her love of mathematics. The limitations would include not only being in a class with students who had completed Grades 7 or 8, but also not being permitted the same degree of freedom on the university campus as her older colleagues.

Tanya's parents had anticipated other maturity-based limitations, such as placing a young student into a learning situation that might require a degree of independent work, including hours upon hours of homework. By requesting an enrichment class, such as Foundations of Algebra, they acknowledged that Tanya must not be pushed out unreasonably. They did not wish to place Tanya, for example, into Algebra I, where she would be expected to have the concentration and planning skills of a high school student and to work at a pace that only very few high school students can maintain.

Yet there are those rare young students who do need to participate in an accelerated class, such as algebra, in order to reach the level of their own pressing mathematical questions, which lie beyond the learning opportunities provided by Foundations of Algebra and which require the fast-paced systematic approach that Secondary Division's Algebra I will provide.

Contrast the Algebra I course description below with the two descriptions above—one (Baker Street Irregulars) providing a transitional experience in Elementary Division and one (Foundations of Algebra) offering exploratory enrichment in Secondary Division. Whereas all three courses most often serve students within a 1- or 2-year age range, their purposes and student experiences are very different. The amount of independent work rises sharply. Consequently, enrollment in Algebra I requires a high score on a standard readiness test, in addition to previous experience, course grade requirements, and a very strong recommendation from the student's mathematics teacher. The content is described as follows:

> This 6-week course provides the equivalent of a standard yearlong high school algebra class. As such, the pace is extremely fast, covering up to 3 weeks of usual instruction per class session. The topics to be covered are: data organization; patterns and graphs; writing and solving equations; numerical, geometric, and algebraic ratios; slopes and rates of change; factoring quadratics; graphing and systems of linear and nonlinear equations; area and sub problems; inequalities; exponents and radicals; and quadratics. The atmosphere of the class is cooperative—the emphasis is on working together. *Homework per class meeting*: 6–10 hours

Placement decisions within Secondary Division are made mostly on the basis of academic preparation and not the age or grade in school of the student. But right away we come up with an exception. A student may be a voracious reader and be very strong in rules of composition, even in fluidity and expression in writing. But regardless of how strong a writing student's skills are and how strong his or her interest is, there is the developmental dimension of maturation, of life experience, that needs to be accounted for when placing a much younger student into a literature class grappling with difficult social and political issues. Whereas we may have the rare sixth grader ready and very enthusiastic to tackle precalculus, we have not yet encountered the same to be true for AP Literature. But room for a necessary exception still exists.

It bears repeating that the learning atmosphere in ATDP classrooms with their wide range of student ages is an accepting and supportive one, so much so that it even surprises us from time to time. For example, the year that a sixth grader was the highest achieving student in his precalculus class, we were delighted and relieved to see the lengths to which his classmates went to assure that he felt safe and secure on a large university campus.

Enough Growing Room with Enough Support

Whereas so broad an age range—5 or 6 years—is unusual in Secondary Division, a 3-year range is not uncommon. In their experience, this is not something that ATDP would wish to approach in Elementary Division, where accelerating a student's placement by even a year is unusual. That does not mean that requests for acceleration are rare. The following example represents quite a few similar requests for exceptions.

The mother of two very bright, socially adept daughters—both of whom were returning for their 3rd summer in Elementary Division—was convinced that Morgan, her younger daughter, needed to be accelerated in writing. Morgan had been placed in a grade-appropriate fourth-grade class. When her mother failed to convince either the program director or ATDP faculty director and head of the UC Berkeley school psychology program Professor Frank Worrell of the desirability of accelerating Morgan into a fifth-grade writing class, the parent proceeded to convince Morgan that she was unhappy in her present class.

Certainly, no one wanted Morgan to be unhappy, and so on the (very slim) off-chance that the ATDP assessment was incorrect, and with the fifth-grade teacher's permission, Morgan proceeded to see whether her needs and expectations might be better met in the fifth-grade class. With the completion of one day in the accelerated placement—and to her mother's chagrin—Morgan asked to return to the fourth-grade class. Morgan's reasoning was sound. She wanted to return because the fourth graders were "doing more interesting things in class, reading better books, and having more fun at recess." This is not surprising, as Morgan was closer to her own cohort in terms of her dreams and interests than she was to the fifth graders, for whom hopes and expectations such as Morgan's were "so last year."

Organizing and Applying Knowledge:
Social Structure, Social Freedom

In the fifth-grade class to which we've just referred there was nonetheless some very important play of its own going on. The class focused on metacognitive aspects of reading and writing, which is a fancy way of saying that the class modeled for its students deep thinking about ideas presented in the books the students read, in their group discussions, and in their own writing. While informal in its setup—gym mats and cushions lined much of the classroom floor and some students stretched out on them as they read new books and thought about what they were reading—the class was very serious in its approach to thinking. So serious, in fact, that sometimes play had to be made compulsory.

With each new book selection, the 25 students in the class recombined into discussion groups of 5 students each. Eventually, everyone had the opportunity to exchange his or her own well-developed ideas with everyone else in a small-group setting. Discussion group times were staggered so that the two instructors might model and lead students in an intellectually rich literary discussion. When one such group just could not, even after several attempts, get an animated discussion going, the teacher gave an unexpected assignment to the five students: "I think that you're having trouble talking with each other because you don't know each other well enough to have a good discussion. You need to go out on the yard to play together for 15 minutes. So, go, play, get to know each other better and then come back in."

In another room, while addressing a serious subject (maybe not practical, but still serious), students in a fifth-grade mathematics class ventured forth to learn all about surface area by collaborating to calculate how much butter would be required to cover the school yard with a 1/8 inch coating. As a given, their instructor stated that the ambient air temperature on the day of the hypothetical butter spreading would be cold enough to assure that butter would not melt on the yard's asphalt paving. The rest of the solution needed to be figured out by the students, who quickly realized that they couldn't just approach the yard as a rectangle, since it had several parts in a variety of shapes. With their teacher and her assistant in the role of facilitators, the students ran around the yard, separated themselves into teams, assigned themselves to investigate different parts of their task, shared information, refined their thinking, and figured it out. All left for the day confident in the knowledge that they knew how much butter they'd need to cover the yard. Oh yes, and also confident that they know how to calculate the surface area of irregularly shaped figures.

EXPLORATION AND PURPOSEFUL LEARNING AREN'T JUST FOR KIDS: INVITING NOVICE TEACHERS INTO THE CONVERSATION

Thus far we hope we have shown the benefits, in terms of deep discipline-specific learning and joyous play experiences, that Elementary Division offers to its students. It also offers similar experiences and benefits to an additional group: instructional associates. Each classroom has at least two significant adults, the lead instructor and an instructional associate. Instructional associate positions were created to serve two purposes, one of which is to have a sufficiently low student-to-teacher ratio to permit students and their teacher to get to know each other in so few days. ATDP staff decided that 12:1 would both provide opportunities for individual attention and also permit more students to be invited into ATDP than could be served by one teacher.

The second purpose was to provide novice teachers with an opportunity to replicate for themselves parts of ATDP students' experiences. ATDP sought to provide novice teachers the experience of teaching in an ideal classroom. ATDP's concern was and continues to be that the competencies and regulations that currently govern the contents of teacher education programs focus on negative conditions and circumstances, thus severely limiting views of classrooms and students. Certainly, all of the conditions against which state-required competencies wish to arm new teachers do most certainly exist. However, such preparation provides few if any opportunities for novice teachers to interact in concert with the elements that comprise a wonderful classroom working in concert.

ATDP wants novice teachers to experience the rich learning enjoyed so much by ATDP's students—the kind of learning described by a novice science teacher working at Bank Street College with Professor Don Cook:

> "Science in this way [as taught by Cook] is so engaging that *we became people with scientific habits of mind*. We get excited by wonderful ideas and do things that enable us to construct our own knowledge. *We learn to believe in ourselves*." (in Cook, 2000, p. 5)

Cook helps his novice teacher to be able to anticipate how terrific a classroom experience can be for both students and teachers. He teaches novice teachers to aim for that experience in all of their teaching. ATDP's hope is that novice teachers will take their experiences, generalize and customize them, and put them into operation anywhere their teaching career takes them.

Good Teaching: When One Size Does Fit All

Donald Schorr, a former ATDP instructional associate, wrote to the ATDP director after completing 3 years of teaching in a low-income, problem-riddled community isolated by two freeways and some train tracks from the very prosperous communities nearby and light-years away from them in terms of educational outcomes. He wrote a long, very reflective, letter highlighting some differences between his own teaching experiences and those of most of his colleagues at school. He said that he credits his experiences in Elementary Division classrooms with providing him an alternate vision of what a classroom should be in a school with characteristics "like his." He wrote that his mission was to convince administrators and his colleagues that classrooms "such as theirs" should strive to replicate the environment and activities of the ATDP classrooms in which he had assisted and in which he had collaborated on curricula and lessons. "All students thrive in classrooms like those [he had enjoyed] at ATDP."

Donald concluded that one of the most important lessons he had learned at ATDP is that there are not separate pedagogies for separate groups. Rather, through his own experiences he had learned that there is

> something called good teaching. And there's only one group. It's called "students." Not only that, but I learned that all groups learn best through multiple learning modes, that all students must be provided with a structure for learning, and that it's an excellent thing when a classroom is abuzz with purposeful chatter, with kids intent their own learning activity, and where everyone has a good giggle a few times each day.

Teaching Novice Teachers About the Seriousness of Playing

Donald singled out the melodrama course in which he had assisted as an especially good example. The text used for this course for third graders was based on the "Winsome Winnie" tale from Stephen Leacock's 1921 book *Winsome Winnie and Other New Nonsense Novels.* In the ATDP class, Winsome Winnie's story is performed by the students in a fully costumed (homemade) melodramatic production to grateful audiences of students, family members, and friends. The language of the text is filled with puns and the super-proper talk of would-be-proper characters. The vocabulary and the language of the class would be considered too sophisticated or esoteric for third graders, and most certainly would be deemed "not relevant to today's heterogeneous student population."

Not only are such claims untrue, but they just might be the reason that master teacher Flossie Lewis selected this text. Lewis uses melodrama as a way of permitting students to learn to savor the possibilities of word play, of experiencing humor, even irony. To do so while dancing the waltz, as do her students, makes it easier to take leaps of many kinds, and certainly defuses many students' concerns about their own abilities, about performing, about fitting in, and a whole host of other worries students have.

Flossie Lewis, who at 80-plus years is still exhausting class after class of writing students at the university, points out that all groups of children use affected speech in their play as they take on any role. The affectation varies, but regardless, it is certainly lofty—be it lofty hip-hop, or lofty Victorian, or the pretend parlance of characters from mythology. Flossie maintains that the more precise or specialized the language used, in context and with scaffolding from the teacher, the more delighted are the students, who then use each new word to fill out even more their detailed images of subjects, topics, and characters.

In our example of the trials and tribulations faced by our dear little orphan-in-the-storm Winnie, Flossie Lewis uses drama, language, and dance as ways to encourage students to suspend disbelief and enter without preconception a new world of language usage. From there, with differences bridged by engaging play, students learn to identify affect and laugh at pompous characters. They recognize and play with manners from other eras and places, and in 3 weeks they learn more literary analysis and interpretation than they might through 2 years or more of direct instruction in school.

This is not Flossie's secret. It's not ATDP's secret either. Rafe Esquith (2003) tells wonderful stories about brand-new English learners, sixth-grade students recently arrived from Korea, Central America, Vietnam, the Philippines, and Thailand performing in *Macbeth*:

> I have a plan to help them with English. I love Shakespeare. . . . I ask the kids if any of them would like to stay after school for an extra two hours a day to improve their English. . . . I tell the parents that by learning English, their children can have better lives.
>
> Five students and their parents bought into the plan. These five children loved putting in the extra time and loved learning about Shakespeare. At first, their peers made fun of them. . . . But these five were having so much fun learning that many of their peers wondered if maybe they were missing something. Within two weeks, I had twenty-eight of them working with me on *Macbeth*. (p. 111)

Selection In, Selection Out: Gatekeepers

Of course, there's no particular magic in selecting to perform either *Winnie* or *Macbeth*. But they and all other similarly rich esoteric activities provide to students the badge of bona fide insider, of the one who has been invited into and joined that most exclusive academic club—that club where members play with words and ideas and dream about things that others will never even hear or have a thought about. While membership is exclusive, invitations are easily extended and are most frequently quickly accepted. Phillip Levien understands the importance of belonging to the exclusive club to students in his English Language Development Program ("Teachers Who ROCK," 2006). He calls Shakespeare a "gatekeeper" author, a symbol of things inaccessible and as such, "bearding the bard" becomes a proof of mastery and membership (p. 13).

In Chapter 4, we are going to carry this idea of "gatekeepers" forward to examine it closely within a variety of contexts—social, economic, political, and academic. We will also look at gates and fences that can be removed and replaced by inclusive communities. As we cautioned at the very beginning, and as we've shown you repeatedly, we don't have any secret answers. But we do offer a different look at what prevents so many of our children from gaining the academic experience they'd delight in having and would thrive on. We also provide a different picture of the components of creating an "ATDP in every classroom," and we carry that notion through the rest of the book.

CHAPTER FOUR

Every Child's Right: Academic Talent Development in All Communities and Classrooms

OVER THE PREVIOUS THREE CHAPTERS, we've shown that growing rather than mining academic talent benefits all. We have shown the advantages of all of us learning from and teaching one another. In this chapter, we move the conversation to a discussion of the broad social and educational circumstances that either prevent or support the growing of academic talent.

In order to show barriers against educating "all of our children together" and then to highlight social and educational conditions that support educational achievement, we have divided the chapter into three parts. First, we present an overview of education as it presently appears inside and outside of school, pointing out some historic barriers to academic talent development. We then deconstruct some ideas and conditions that create or exacerbate problems presently preventing academic talent development for many children and youth. Finally, we identify beliefs and conditions required for offering an ATDP-type of education to all children, in all classrooms.

In Chapters 5 and 6 we will present some examples of how well things work when academic talent development is available by choice, rather than by chance.

STARTING WITH THINGS AS THEY ARE

We've shown in each previous chapter, via ATDP student experiences, that all children and youth have the same educational and social needs. Those seeking to mine academic talent ignore this point and regard talent as an inborn or somehow static characteristic, something that students either already possess or don't. Some like Charles Murray (2007 a, b, c) identify academic talent by generating lists of students whom they presume, because of their high IQs, to absorb knowledge effortlessly. Others identify academic talent by generating lists of those kinds of students whom they report to be members of "model minorities," and whom they assume by virtue of birth, are not only able but also ready for exceptional performance (Petersen, 1966; Wu, 2002). Still others make lists of groups in society who they assume do not know, or even want to know, enough to make it academically.

Such lists of false groupings are perpetuated by widely held misperceptions about society, people, and who does and does not learn. The problems we are about to present are seriously exacerbated when these false groupings are played out in public policy and in classrooms. Too often the false groupings remain unquestioned and unexamined. Decision makers too frequently treat false groupings as if they were facts, then persist in basing their decisions regarding schooling and education on them (e.g., see Logan, 2002; Anderson, quoted in Perry, Steele, & Hilliard, 2003, p. 62). The results are brutal and most punishing for those with the fewest resources.

Carolyn M. Callahan's (2005) assessment of the current state of academic talent development for all students nationwide is succinct and direct, so we use it here to set the parameters within which we'll conduct our exploration:

> Inadequate opportunities for talent development are the result of erroneous beliefs translated into detrimental practice. The two beliefs that mitigate against adequate talent development are: (a) the belief that it is the role of gifted and talented programs to serve only those children that parents bring to the school door "signed, sealed, and delivered" as gifted [or academically well developed in our context here]; and (b) inherent beliefs about the low capabilities of poor and minority children . . . the more common belief is that there are few students who come from ethnic minority groups or from families in poverty who are capable of developing into gifted children and adults or of exhibiting gifted behaviors. In fact, there is a strong, erroneous belief that most of these children are so lacking in prerequisite basic skill or abilities that such development is highly unlikely. (pp. 1–2; see also Clasen, 1994; Dusek & Joseph, 1983; Frasier, Garcia, & Passow, 1995; McCarty, Lynch, Wallace, & Benally, 1991)

The Needs Are the Same; the Resources Aren't

ATDP's own experience shows over and over that all students acquire necessary skills and knowledge in the same ways—they learn, practice, and apply them. The learning process is the same for all. That process requires a combination of modeled behaviors, personal and vicarious experiences supported by direct instruction, and lots and lots of practice, including rehearsal and performance (Gabelko, 1991). While the needs are similar, the available resources to satisfy them are becoming even more disparate over time.

ATDP's own neighborhood, the San Francisco Bay Area, provides an example of the growing disparity among ethnic and racial groups and makes explicit what presently is blocking existing possibilities and is closing off access to others. According to the 2000 census, the Bay Area shows some of the greatest disparities in the nation. Not only have income disparities grown over the previous decade, but also the ability of African American and Hispanic families to improve their family situation has declined even further, well behind White and Asian families. "Due to residential segregation, Blacks and Hispanics are [now] less able to move to better neighborhoods. . . . [The neighborhood gap] . . . was growing faster for the most affluent Blacks and Hispanics (compared to Whites with similar incomes) than for those close to the poverty line" (Logan, 2002, p. 1).

Concomitant with that, in 2004 the codirector of the Harvard Civil Rights Project reported that since 1990 resegregation rates have been on the rise nationwide (Lester, 2004). Meanwhile, the achievement gap, after years of having moved toward closing (Grissmer, Flanagan, & Williamson, 1998), began widening at the same time as resegregation rates began climbing again (Ferguson, 2002), and neither trend shows any signs that it's about to decline (see also Apple, 1996, p. 73).

The "Neighborhood Gap" represents the quality of life as it is associated not only with income, but also with inequalities in public schools, safety, environmental quality, and public health (Logan, 2002, Tables 1 and 2, pp. 2, 4). In examining the gap, we see that even in situations where there is seeming parity between and among groups—such as family income and concomitant opportunities for high-quality schooling—Black and Hispanic families in particular are still stigmatized and placed at great disadvantage. Consequently, many students have far fewer academic resources available to them than it seems to those who take family income as the indicator of access to possibilities without consideration of color (Gosa & Alexander, 2007).

The situations and conditions we present here and the concepts we discuss are not esoteric or even unusual. In fact some are so usual that they've become invisible or are ignored. So, let's reexamine, redefine, and recombine new and old ideas in an effort to see things more clearly.

Reframing the Issue: Effects of "One Lens Only" Views

Recall Carolina, (see Chapter 2) who came to ATDP from a low-income rural community where low scores on the Academic Performance Index (API) and lower performing students were not hitting the mark, where unemployment and school dropout rates were very high, as was teen pregnancy. Carolina accurately presents herself as a high-achieving scholar, directly connected to everyone else at ATDP. Simultaneously, she sees herself as directly connected to her home community.

Despite her academic and personal success as well as those of her siblings and friends, Carolina's views of possibilities for educating presently marginalized groups are rarely reflected or considered in terms of common education practice. Rather, the general thinking reverts to previously held conclusions about towns like hers and API scores like the ones at her alma mater. Even though counter information is easily available, it's rarely considered because Carolina and many others like her are identified by a view through a single lens, the one that focuses only on ethnicity and social class.

Within a "one lens only" framework, Carolina is seen as an anomalous member of a Central California farm-working community, rather than as a typical ATDP student. While both assessments are valid, only one—the one of her as an anomaly—will be used as the basis of many important assumptions and generalizations about an appropriate education. That view does not even consider information provided by Carolina, or her peers who have come to ATDP over the past two decades. That single-lens view is at great odds with what has been seen by their college professors. It would not even be recognized by their current supervisors at departments of regional and city planning, international engineering firms, or the school districts in which they teach.

Really wrong assumptions further marginalize students. This single-lens frame of reference is based on a belief that there is an underclass uniformly defined by ethnicity and race. The single lens identifies individuals by racial or ethnic stereotypes, and defines both group and individual only in terms of stigmas (Dubose, 2005; Valenzuela, 1999). As such, both the groups and individuals within them are represented as repositories of and for problems. When educators, policy makers, and the general public use the one-lens view they clump members of marginalized groups into a single, uniform community defined by racial and ethnic stereotypes.

At the same time, the assumption is that Whites and Asians (though less so than Whites) can and do belong to multiple communities that are complex, multidimensional, and divergent. Whites and Asians are viewed simultaneously as individuals, as members of a democratic society, and members of the primary reference group from which they hail. Whites and Asians are expected to be found anywhere along the political spectrum, to have any of a long list of religious affiliations, to be smart or not, to have professional standing or not, and to be athletic or downright klutzy, and so on.

It's no surprise that misidentification of large groups of students represented in the schools causes problems for all of us and ruins academic possibilities and curtails expectations for eager students, all of them complex individuals, none of whom can be seen accurately through a single lens. The groups to which students belong are multiple and multidimensional. We want to assert that "admittance into one group does not necessarily mean that individuals have to relinquish membership in previous or other groups" (Dawson & Chatman, 2001). Pollock (2004) adds that "students bend" these "simple" race categories by sometimes moving between them, sometimes embracing them, and sometimes rejecting them. Nevertheless, the membership categories remain "intact" and relatively stable. Yet this vital piece of the achievement puzzle is almost universally ignored, while the stereotypes persist (see also Horvat & O'Connor, 2006, p. 29).

More examples of harm caused by "one lens only." In a *Wall Street Journal* article, reporter David Golden (2004) presents prevailing sentiments, formed and acted upon in the "one lens only" presentation of "facts." Golden discloses clearly how thinking about possibilities for talent development nationwide is buried under layer upon layer of spurious connections. These wrong connections stereotype and stigmatize accomplished and passionate students because they remain unusual within a particular interpretation of some unnamed context. Golden frames the "problem with equity," as presented to him by members of the gifted education communities in the towns he writes about, like this:

> Around the country and especially in the South, new tests are propelling more minority students into predominantly White gifted-education programs. Proponents applaud what they say is an overdue easing of racial disparities in gifted education, stressing that the special classes can open greater opportunities for Blacks, Hispanics, and Native Americans.
>
> But it's not that simple. By changing the standards for gifted education, traditionalists say, school districts seeking classroom equity are undermining academic excellence. Some minority students identified as gifted are actually struggling in regular classes, raising questions about whether the new criteria accurately gauge academic ability. And some school-board members, teachers, and parents complain that the admission of more students, both White and minority has watered down the quality of gifted programs. (p. 1)

We see that those speaking in Golden's article have already linked "race" plus "equity" to "the diluting of high standards." As "evidence" of such diluting, they point directly to lower achieving students, identifying them as having questionable ability. The speakers state that they're suspicious of new indicators that disclose academic talent among groups of people they assume have none. The speakers further see the use of new indicators for new groups of students being wrongly placed into programs established for "real" gifted students. The result of this applied false evidence of poor performance is linked to "academic ability," but not to prior schooling, to which it is actually directly linked and of which it is a product.

If the evaluations made by those interviewed in Golden's article were true, then it would also hold true that if we place students who haven't yet completed algebra into a calculus class, their poor performance could serve as evidence of the students' lack of mathematical ability, without reference to the kind of preparation our students have not had. Previous educational achievement is unaccounted for and present educational needs are not considered, let alone planned for (Horvat & O'Connor, 2006, pp. 177–182).

Again, unrelated statements are linked in support of already-held incorrect judgments of what constitutes ability or how it is developed. Consequently, the whole universe that exists between present performance and possibilities of achievement is disregarded, ignored, or invisible. Yet it is within that universe that learning, equity, and possibilities exist.

JUST A LITTLE DECONSTRUCTION

If we use an old lens to view the conditions, experiences, and frames of mind we've presented thus far, we will see a clearer-than-usual picture of the roots and consequences of the barriers to educational equity we're examining. The old lens was presented over half-a-century ago by Gordon W. Allport (1954/1979), the same year the *Brown v. Board of Education of Topeka* decision was handed down.

Allport asked us to be aware of the thinking process through which prejudice and stereotypes persist and regenerate. He showed how the process of selection of information to be presented is focused and interpreted, then used to present as a conclusion a belief that's actually a prejudgment. Stereotypes are the prejudgments on which prejudice is based.

We know from history and from personal experiences that stereotypes stand and continue to be replicated generation after generation. They're easily perpetuated, since they come preconceived, require no thinking, and can serve to withhold social, political, and economic capital from those being stereotyped (Gabelko & Michaelis, 1981, pp. 21, 53).

That stereotype becomes prejudice when it is acted upon. That prejudice becomes discrimination when people use their unexamined prejudgments to hold members of a group at a disadvantage solely because they are identified as part of the stereotyped group. The discriminated-against group members are harmed not because of anything that they have done but because partial information or faulty generalizations have been used in determining the basis for actions.

As Martin Grotjahn put it in 1954, "it is easier—and probably cheaper—to smash an atom than a prejudice" (p. 605). When that prejudice takes the form of an action, it becomes a public matter. But it doesn't show us what to do.

Let's use the "Allport lens" as ATDP employs it, to reexamine some presumed but easily avoided impediments to developing academic talent and then use it again to disclose actual barriers that are frequently overlooked. In this way, we hope to make learning possibilities explicit, investigate the importance of particular kinds of peer effects, and locate the kind of opportunities that close achievement gaps. Once again the necessity of considering "all of our children together" is paramount.

Not Talking About Social Class and Race
Doesn't Make Things Better: Families Want to Talk

In profound and devastating ways, color and social class still matter in the United States (Lester, 2004; Pollack, 2004, 2005). When they are discussed at all in mixed-group forums the conversations are marked by circumlocution. Mica Pollock (2004) points out that much of this avoidance is motivated by a fear of being branded as a racist or a belief that talking about race will only inflame under-the-surface tensions. Those who have such fears tend to try assuaging them with statements such as "it would serve only to make matters even worse if we talk about race." Yet, when educators avoid the topic of race, it's detrimental for all (p. 121).

We wonder, already knowing the extent to which teachers and school officials will go to avoid candid conversations about race, whether community psychologist Clark McKown was astounded as well as delighted by the strength of the positive response he received when he asked ethnically diverse groups of parents whether they would permit their 6- to 10-year-old children to participate in interviews about race and stereotypes. One administrator at an outside-of-school program told McKown that he was welcome to extend the invitations, but, based on her long years of experience, no adults would want to talk about race, much less want to have their children discuss stereotypes of self and others (McKown, personal communication, May 25, 2001). Yet families—African American and Hispanic especially—were so eager to contribute to the development of knowledge about the world as they and their families experience it that the line of parents wanting to sign up must have been a block long.

Participating family members whose children are stigmatized by stereotypes about race and ethnicity were eager to enter the conversation and stated their eagerness to contribute to the good that would result from such discussions. Many of the adult family members came to these conversations with deep, deep understandings of stereotypes and prejudices. They knew firsthand the harm caused. Their candid participation made important contributions to knowledge, just as they hoped it would.

Effects of Stereotyping Are Disclosed Through Conversation

Australian researcher Ninetta Santoro (2005) adds a big piece to the puzzle when she emphasizes that "Some teachers fall into the trap of assigning fixed and 'essential' characteristics to the ethnic groups and can indiscriminately use these characteristics to explain the educational achievements (or otherwise) of a group of students, or to justify particular classroom practices. If *difference* is the *only lens* through which teachers see students, teachers cannot know their students or address their intellectual needs" (p. 2).

Santoro's statement is clearly exemplified by schooling experiences of two longtime ATDP students, both African American males, from different socioeconomic backgrounds. Shawn is 13 years old and his family's income falls within the upper-middle-class rank, even in the Bay Area; both parents are university educated at the graduate level (as were their parents) and are in professional careers. The family strongly supports the visual and performing arts and Shawn's parents are expert in both. Shawn particularly enjoys mathematics, and via his ATDP studies performs at least a full year ahead of his public school district's stated expectations for his grade level.

Shawn's parents have tried for years to have him appropriately placed into accelerated and honors mathematics classes. They have repeatedly been turned back at the classroom, school, and school-district levels. The stated reason is that their son, who is one of very few Black students at his public school, is not "ready" to accelerate.

Most recently, his school principal said that she would not recognize Shawn's ATDP achievements because it's not in Shawn's interest to accelerate; he should not be "pushed." Yet other students—non-Black—who perform at the same level as he in their ATDP math classes are frequently "pushed" by the same school district, even at the same school. The district-level personnel state that, in their district, the decision regarding acceleration is up to the site administrator, adding that they must warn Shawn's parents against putting too much academic pressure on their child. No similar caution is presented to other families.

Isaiah, another ATDP student, lives full-time with his retired grand-mother in a subsidized-housing apartment. Isaiah attends a public school where over 70% of the students qualify for free or reduced cost lunch and about 80% of the students self-identify as African American. While Isaiah is a year younger than Shawn, they attended the same ATDP algebra class. In other words, Isaiah's mathematics achievements are at least 2 years ahead of grade-level expectations and probably 5 years ahead of his class-mates at school.

Isaiah's report card is one long list of A grades. His classes are all keyed to the year-end high-stakes exam, on which his performance is stellar. Yet it seems that because of his race and family-income level, Isaiah is con-fronted by a barrier invisible to most observers who comment on how fabu-lous it is that an African American male from a disadvantaged background is "just thriving at school." As with Shawn, the school's focus is on how African American male students are expected to behave and perform, and the consensus at school is that Isaiah, by color, is doing brilliantly. Isaiah is frequently commended by the principal for his excellent performance in class and on standardized tests.

Isaiah, whether because of very strong aptitude or lots of practice doing mental arithmetic, performs all calculations in his head, and at his school his answers are correct just about every time. However, both Isaiah and his family were similarly surprised when Isaiah, who ordinarily completes his homework (which has almost exclusively been arithmetic calculations) in a very few minutes, was now taking so very long to complete his home-work at ATDP. He had no time left to do anything else; he was even eating lunch and dinner at his desk.

Teacher, ATDP counselor, and family agreed that something was wrong. His family sought a reason or reasons for the difficulties Isaiah con-fronted and said they were very worried that "Isaiah might not be competi-tive in a mixed-race classroom." Hours and days were devoted to tutorial and academic counseling before the family could be convinced that the dif-ficulties Isaiah was experiencing were not the result of his abilities but of his educational history.

Up to that point, Isaiah had had no prior experience with mathemat-ics that he couldn't compute in his head. ATDP was his first exposure to complex math concepts, ones that required thinking time as well as a paper and pencil to complete. This reframing of the problem posed a dilemma for both Isaiah and ATDP. He needed constant support to accept the idea that there was no prize for completing things first, and even more sup-port to convince him that he now needed to attend to every word the teacher and members of his class had to say. While it wasn't something any 12-year-old might do preferentially, Isaiah had to admit that he could certainly do what was needed.

Both Shawn and Isaiah exemplify reasons for ATDP's concern over the "one lens only" effect of returning talented mathematics students to an environment in which their minds are permitted to idle and where, unless their circumstances change, students like Shawn will continue to have the import of his performance deflated and Isaiah will continue to be highly praised for his almost perfect memory.

Stop Mining Academic Talent; Start Growing It

For ATDP, a seemingly obvious step toward developing an accurate view of students is to help teachers, schools, and school districts to move away from conventional ways of mining academic talent and to show them other ways—ways of growing talent. That means that we need to change the questions we ask when we seek students to attend academic talent development programs. We need questions regarding students to be behaviorally based.

When asked to nominate candidates for ATDP, even the most dedicated faculties at schools in marginalized communities frequently reply: "In this school, in this room, we don't have academically talented children. We all try our very best, including the kids, but it's not that kind of a school." Asking the same old mining question of "Who in your class is academically talented?" will produce the same old response—to quote Callahan (2005), there are no students here who can be "signed, sealed, and delivered." But the situation changes when we ask different questions.

Asking the right questions can trump good intentions. How could hardworking, dedicated teachers have so little faith in their own students' prospects for academic success? How could they not identify academically talented students? Or, is that the wrong question? Is it even reasonable to expect a novel response to a stereotypical, or at least typical, question: "Whom do you nominate for participation in a university-based academic talent development program?"

When at first ATDP staff replied, also with the best of intentions, "But academic talent is distributed across the whole population," this approach neither succeeded in furthering relationships with teachers and schools nor in inviting more students from marginalized groups to join the program. All ATDP's encouragement did was to activate stereotypes of "academically talented children."

Useful data, not conclusionary responses. Since 1991, in ATDP's "regular" application process, ATDP asks teachers to report the frequency of student behaviors identified by teachers and researchers as typical of children and youth who are a good match for the program. For example, "Which children in your third grade ask the most questions?" "Which children have strong interests and stay on task for a long time?" "Who in your classroom gets jokes most quickly and who likes to play with words?" These and similar questions have brought more useful and positive responses from teachers and school administrators, across all groups. It is a great help that such questions could honestly be answered by teachers who knew their students and carefully observed their learning behaviors in the classroom.

High-Achieving Members of Minority Groups Are Also Subjected to Stereotyping and Discrimination

Franklin Johnstone is a perfect example of someone who, all throughout school, outside of school, and at ATDP did everything right. He was always a brilliant, dedicated student, a standard higher than others around him. Yet his schooling experiences provide a graphic example of conditions—barriers—that students from minority groups continue to face, regardless of the excellence they bring with them to the classroom.

Except for the year that he competed in an international martial arts competition, Franklin Johnstone participated in ATDP every year between Grades 2 and 11. By Grade 9 he had already completed ATDP's most challenging courses, so he became a paid tutor, a mentor, and an assistant instructor in various mathematics and computer classes. His heart was in the principles on which his martial arts is based: courtesy, integrity, perseverance, self-control, and an indomitable spirit. His loyalty to his sensei was astounding, so while he worked at ATDP he also helped to teach martial arts. He offered this service in exchange for the private coaching he received from his sensei.

Because his mother was disabled and every penny was needed for the family to survive, Franklin also carried a third part-time job during the summer. During the school year he worked only two jobs because he attended a community college at night.

Franklin and his mother lived a very long commute from Berkeley in a small apartment situated in a middle-class community. Their town was more expensive than tony, more blue-collar than many of the residents would admit. Mrs. Johnstone believed that her son would have a better chance there than he would in an all-Black neighborhood and school. In his school, Franklin was one of fewer than a dozen African American students in his grade, and once he reached middle and high school was frequently the only person of color in his classes. The friends he made were through his martial arts; he made none through his school and few at ATDP.

At ATDP, according to the director and all of his teachers there, intellectually Franklin was one of those students one never forgets—that top 1% they ask you about on recommendation forms. For example, in order for him to learn as much mathematics as he felt he needed to, during one summer at ATDP, he attempted both a course in high school geometry and a second course in precalculus, earning an A in each. Thus in the fall he could take calculus at the community college.

All this, and at grade level, too! At his high school, Franklin did very well, in terms of his marks and his test scores: very well, and in grade-appropriate classes, too. His teachers frequently told Mrs. Johnstone how proud they were of Franklin. "Okay, then what about granting him credit for his accomplishments at ATDP and permitting him to enroll in advanced and accelerated classes based on his academic achievements in the program?" (Is this starting to sound familiar?)

"Well, no, that is out of the question," according to the counselor, the head counselor, the vice-principal, and the principal, claiming that such a move was not only against district policy but also not in Franklin's best interest. Mrs. Johnstone asked to see a copy of the policy, but it turned out to be one of those "unwritten facts." Mrs. Johnstone didn't have the resources to pursue the fight further.

But Franklin wouldn't permit his education to be stalled or held back. At Franklin's request and with his mother's permission, he began attending the local community college in the evening. Yes, it was counter to (written) policy to have a high-schooler attend without the written consent of his guidance counselor, but the community college made an exception based on his test scores and his mother's agreement to be present on campus whenever he was in attendance at night school.

Mrs. Johnstone did not want Franklin's schooling situation to be discussed outside of the family and insisted that if the ATDP director were to attempt to intercede it would make matters worse for Franklin at high school and might even get the community college into trouble for having made an exception. So, throughout high school, Franklin attended regular high school during the day, worked two jobs in the afternoon and on weekends, and attended community college in the evening. On top of that, somehow he continued to pursue his martial arts.

Before the end of 11th grade, he had completed 2 years of college-level mathematics and 2 years of college-level laboratory science. Of course, the SATs were no problem for him and his scores reflected his academic achievement at community college, not high school. Franklin earned offers of full 4-year scholarships to four very prestigious private universities in different regions of the United States. What a happy ending for one who had traveled such a steep path, no? Well, that's just it. It is no; well and truly it is.

University academics posed no problem, but the school culture did. To no one's surprise, the academics posed no problem for Franklin during his first year at college, which was also his first year away from home. In fact, one could safely say that Franklin had arrived at college "signed, sealed, and delivered." He found his classes challenging but not difficult, and he even had time to continue his martial arts. And yet, when the ATDP director called Mrs. Johnstone to inquire whether she and Franklin might be willing to speak at the upcoming Secondary Division orientation, Mrs. Johnstone said that she would not even bring up the matter with Franklin. His year had been so horrible that neither of them was willing to bring any attention to him or to tell anyone about how it had been almost close to impossible to survive his first year at college.

Franklin's first and subsequent years, except academically and except for the friendships he maintained through martial arts, were torture. Franklin had been as welcomed into university life by his classmates as were the Black students into Little Rock's Central High School in 1955. Remember, though, that Franklin was attempting to make his way many decades later.

He endured harassment and "practical jokes," such as having his computer stolen from his dorm room and its memory erased. He was openly mocked by fellow undergraduates for his appearance and his modest family resources. There were other experiences, but these are the ones that Mrs. Johnstone shared with the ATDP director.

The problem wasn't so much the behavior of professors; most paid him little personal attention. A few voiced their surprise at the superior quality of his work ("amazing for a student from a public high school at a university like this"), and a few even made him feel welcome in their offices. But his peers and the faceless others made it clear in every way that Franklin was an unwelcome interloper, an interloper who was academically stellar.

Nonetheless, Franklin graduated from the university, and he did so with distinction. But at what personal cost? Now some years out of college, he is a ranking official in national security. This the ATDP director knows from one conversation, a few years ago, with Mrs. Johnstone.

Pennsylvania State University Professor Beverly J. Vandiver advanced our understanding of Franklin's situation, when in her capacity as head counselor and researcher at ATDP, she shed light on Johnstone's educational experiences as clear examples of why it has to be "all of our children, all of us, together within a democratic framework." In a recent conversation with the ATDP director, Vandiver said:

> I think institutional, peer, and teacher effects contribute to the development or impairment of achievement for racial minority youth. The fact is that belonging to a civic and intellectual community strengthens the belief that "I can achieve" and buffers the cultural ecological damage that pervades the academic experience of many children. The damage is hierarchical, collateral, and reciprocal in that it makes all of our communities weaker, weakens the effort of future children, and takes a heavy toll on possibilities of richness for the current teacher-peer community.

We add one more piece to our puzzle when we recognize that noncognitive indicators are every bit as powerful as cognitive ones in the development of academic talent. Franklin Johnstone's experiences have demonstrated their importance. To state things in the affirmative, in speaking of social contexts that foster outstanding academic and personal growth among gifted youth, Laurence J. Coleman (2005) says:

> My contention is that ordinary interactions in special contexts are pivotal to the development of talent and are more significant for advanced development than are an individual's abilities. I believe that noncognitive behaviors manifested in those settings are momentous indicators of the power of those special contexts in furthering development. (p. 114)

Students Learn What They Live: The Dangers of Stereotypes

We do not present Franklin Johnstone's school history as an example of what happens to every African American student who ventures into nontraditional realms. But we do know that many parts of his experience have an all too familiar ring to many and aren't merely rooted in family lore, tales from the olden days, or circumstances that changed over fifty years ago. Franklin's experiences are pretty much what students like him learn to anticipate, be it firsthand or vicariously.

Partly because Franklin Johnstone's story has an individual's name and face on it, partly because his story shows what can and often does happen to a young person who has done everything more-than-right, Franklin Johnstone's experience is an important one for everyone concerned with schooling to know. An awareness of his experiences serves to contextualize worries held and acted upon today by members of racial minority groups. From the Johnstone family's perspective, let's proceed to look at some consequences of negative ascriptions and experiences as they affect individuals and institutions.

Faulty assumptions, foolish conclusions. With some frequency we hear or read statements that in minority group communities, middle and high school students who might otherwise be interested in academics and in the life of the mind are placed in jeopardy by being acknowledged as smart or good students. The faulty assumption on which such statements are based is that peers take negative sanctions against classmates who are smart or good students for "acting white," and thus betraying the cause of their own people by trying to join the enemy. In other words, in order to maintain their own identity, racial and ethnic minority youth assume a stance in opposition to the behaviors expected by social institutions such as the schools, thus forming an *oppositional culture.*

We suggest that this view of an oppositional culture—as it is held by many school administrators, classroom teachers, and others in the general public—is predicated on a misconception of John Ogbu's important oppositional culture frameworks (OCFs) (Ogbu, 2003, 2004; Ogbu & Simons, 1998).

Misapplication of OCFs creates the false belief that threats of negative peer sanctions for being smart and doing well in school should somehow be assigned different import across groups of students. In some conversations about achievement gaps and appropriate schooling for African American and Hispanic children and youth, preventing negative peer sanctions is given central focus by more than a few misinformed school personnel wondering aloud whether it isn't dangerous to place African American students in jeopardy by forcing them into visibly academically demanding situations, which may provoke reprisals from their peers. Such interpretations are generalized to mean that these are somehow minority problems and thus fall into a category that, for example, makes thinking about African American students different from thinking about White or Asian students.

Those who misapply OCFs rely on information obtained almost exclusively from reports of low-achieving students (Horvat & O'Connor, 2006, p. 27). Ogbu himself and many others have warned against misinterpreting and overapplying OCFs too broadly.

Let's reframe the conversation. Horvat and O'Connor (2006) reframe for us the debate on Black student achievement. In the preface, for example, Carol D. Lee critiques one of the many variations on the "pathology in the culture" hypothesis: that among African American students, doing well in school is equated with and disdained as "acting White," creating perverse incentives and disincentives for low-performing and high-performing students alike. Lee disagrees:

> First, it is an ahistorical argument. Second it reifies old theories about black inferiority, and, in so doing, invites discussion about what is fundamentally an absurd question. (p. x)

In her examination of nondominant forms of cultural capital (NDCC), Carter (2005) demonstrates that poor African American youth both value educational achievement and at the same time seek to gather peer respect via accruing cultural capital acquired by demonstrating their faithfulness to African American youth culture.

When rapper Snoop Dogg, who was speaking about a college women's basketball team at Rutgers University, said that he wanted it understood that African American high achievers are due particular respect within the rap and greater Black communities, both what he said and the way in which he said it are borne out as true by ethnographic research. Snoop Dogg said, "[Rappers] are not talking about no collegiate basketball girls who have made it to the next level in education and in sports" (Reid, 2007, p. 1).

Effects of stereotypes on academic planning. ATDP's faculty director Frank Worrell (2003) points out that, "in addition to the reasons students may *choose* to underachieve [e.g., oppositional culture], there are some reasons for underachievement that may not be consciously controlled," pointing to stereotyping as the most evident of these reasons (p. 430). Steele and Aronson (1995) demonstrated that African Americans who perform in situations rife with negative stereotypes of themselves showed significantly lower scores in comparison to other African Americans who performed the same tasks in situations where invoked stereotypes are absent (see also Blascovich, Spencer, Quinn, & Steele, 2001; Steele, 1998; Steele & Aronson, 1995).

Clearly, stereotype threat presents a huge barrier to making academic talent development a viable choice for students from educationally marginalized groups. *Stereotype threat* is a pervasive and potentially crippling fear that widely held negative views of their racial or ethnic group will be invoked by others to prevent them from functioning to their full capacities, whether at college, on the job, or even in interpersonal interactions in mixed-group situations (McKown & Weinstein, 2003; Sackett, Hardison, & Cullen, 2004; Steele & Aronson, 1995). These threats are for the most part unacknowledged or unrecognized, but they are pervasive. The question remains. How can we support and encourage students who have to face these fears to develop their academic talents?

In terms of educational planning, we suggest that it is far more important to understand the effect of stereotypes so widely projected that they instill into students deep concerns that there might be truth in these accusations and thus can shake the confidence of the individual. The question then arises for the group and for the individuals whether stereotyped individuals set themselves up for constant assault and even failure by venturing forth against the stereotype. This is a very different proposition from the notion that students assume a stance in opposition to their own culture when venturing forth into academic achievement.

Failing to acknowledge the power of stereotype threat when considering student performance across groups can imply that as some students suffer "minority problems"—such as supposed negative social sanctions for school achievement—they require different considerations and measures. When we acknowledge that all groups admire academic achievement we come to view things quite differently. Now we come to view those who attempt to thwart other students' achievements as just plain bullies. And as soon as we look, we find bullies within and across all groups, and we are left with a different view of a different-than-the-anticipated problem.

Bullying

In elementary school, the prevalence of bullying perpetrated by (yes, that is *by*, not *on*) gifted students is on the increase (Peterson & Ray, 2006, p. 153). Across all groups, name-calling, bullying, and threatening happens in "the absence of significant differences in regard to location, population density, and race/ethnicity" (Nansel et al., 2001). Bullying is universal.

Bullying, we can all agree, is a problem requiring attention whenever it appears. So it is both disappointing and reassuring that Kirk A. Johnson (2000), in examining the 1998 *National Assessment of Educational Progress* database, found that when eighth graders, across racial groups, were asked to agree or disagree with the statement "My friends make fun of people who try to do well in school," the following percentages of students selecting "agree" or "strongly agree" were: White, 22.9%; African American, 23.3%; Hispanic, 29.4%; other, 28.0%. And when we add the relatively new phenomenon of "cyberbullying," which adds the dimension of anonymity for bullies, the potential for nastiness grows exponentially (Wiseman, 2007).

Happily, by high school bullying decreases greatly across all groups, as students grow somewhat more involved in their own business and with their own friends. Furthermore, Ronald Ferguson's (2002) research, conducted in conjunction with the Minority Student Achievement Network, shows that African American students are more likely than their White peers to state that it is important to work hard and get good grades. It is important not to ascribe bullying, its perpetrators or its recipients or its effects, differently across ethnic or social groups.

Just Because Two Statements Are True Independently Doesn't Mean They Can Be Combined

We keep coming up against problems that arise when observations or statements, which may well be accurate separately, when combined with other observations, which may also be accurate, create a false third piece of seeming information. For example, it is true that oppositional culture can play an important, but not always positive, role in marginalized communities. It is also true that there are many incidents of bullying and other negative sanctions being taken among high-achieving students, as well as low-achieving students. Even though both statements may be independently true, the connection isn't between oppositional culture and negative sanctions. When the two are combined they can seriously misinform and precipitate wrong conclusions. In our example, they wrongly shift focus away from serious problems—for example, ill effects on students of being taunted, bullied, and harmed—and onto misinformation regarding cultures.

Wrongly combined, such confusion causes widespread problems in education and frequently blocks opportunities for academic talent development. For example, educators and policy makers send everyone in the wrong direction when unknowingly they connect two independently correct assumptions to form a misleading and incorrect whole. Bridgeman and Wendler in *Characteristics of Minority Students Who Excel on the SAT and in the Classroom* (2005) offer clear examples of how such incorrect connections encourage faulty generalizations.

Their examples permit us to disclose how wrongly combined information derails conversations about barriers blocking academic possibilities of students from marginalized minority groups. They show a real-life example of Simpson's paradox where $1 + 2 \neq 3$ and demonstrate to us why we need a frame of reference that acknowledges paradoxes.

> Overall, African American and Hispanic students are less likely than White students to take challenging courses. Within each score level, however, they are as likely or more likely to take such courses. This is an example of Simpson's paradox. The explanation of the paradox is that the African American and Hispanic students are relatively more numerous at the lower score levels, and fewer advanced courses are taken at these levels. *The problem is not that high-scoring minorities do not take challenging course, but rather that there are too few high-scoring minority students.* (Bridgeman & Wendler, 2005, p. 6; emphasis added)

Let us consider the equation A + B ≠ AB. Thus, even if research reports that A is correct and that research report B is also correct, we cannot assume that they can be combined to form a third report called AB.

We wish to underline the point that unrelated sets of data cannot be assumed to equate. Researchers, policy makers, and administrators should not be able to go unchallenged when they present as conclusions wrongly combined information that then produces potentially dangerous prescriptions, prescriptions that wrongly reinforce stereotypes and furthers stigmas.

Given so many things to ignore, how do we keep from being stymied in our own efforts? How on earth can we ever again move with confidence?

PUTTING THINGS TOGETHER: IT'S ALL ABOUT CONTEXT

Let's start here by showing how the points we've discussed in this chapter thus far are important to us. We reiterate that we are defining the goal of education—in school and out—in terms of the development of judgment and expertise, rather than the more widespread notion of skill competence. We're going to look at our topics within the context of civic culture in order to disclose why it has to be "all of us together." From within the context of civic culture, we'll examine the importance of communities of practice. Then we'll take a new look at "signed, sealed, and delivered," a different kind of peer effect, and together we'll create many possibilities for many, many students.

ATDP's Context

We have examined some barriers preventing all of our children from developing academic talent. Now, we're ready to examine the context required in order to develop and implement our educational goals. To do so, we will identify structures, practices, and beliefs that need to be in place and functioning in order for us to meet our goals.

By focusing on ATDP's evolution, we hope to convince you that there is no need to wait until we can have "an ATDP in every classroom," though that is our ultimate goal, because the process can begin right now, everywhere, and with the resources at hand (remember that ATDP is self-sustaining—that's a benefit of all of our children being together).

Context gives meaning to individual events—be it "signed, sealed, and delivered" (Callahan, 2005) or fear of "watering down gifted programs" (Golden, 2004), or the Johnstone family's experiences with K–16 schooling. ATDP had to identify the appropriate context for bringing all of our children together and then develop and proclaim its own point of view.

Otherwise it would not have been able to do its job; it would not even have known what its job was.

Just believing that the ATDP staff wanted to provide a different kind of rich, challenging education for all students was not sufficient. The ATDP staff needed to work from within an agreed-upon system of fundamental beliefs or a philosophy. Only then could they define their own place and their own job.

Some might say, however, and we certainly do, that public education in the United States has short-circuited this process and has supplanted philosophy with rhetoric, reasoned decisions with ideology. Consequently, many decisions made in the name of the common good are predicated on a process that projects a catchy-phrased conclusion that merely points to sets of marching orders.

We Require a Culture of Democracy

We use the lens of civic culture to examine the "characteristics and pre-conditions of the culture of democracy" (Almond & Verba, 1989, pp. 10–26). Within the civic culture:

> individuals become participants in the political process, but they do not give up their [own orientations]. . . . Furthermore, not only are these earlier orientations [of their own] maintained, but they are congruent with the participant political orientations. . . . Thus attitudes favorable to participation within the political system play a major role in civic culture, but so do such non-political attitudes as trust in other people and social participation in general. (Almond & Verba, 1989, p. 30)

Be it regarding national issues or one's own education, it's vital that we view participation in the civic culture as being requisite for full membership in American society. Consequently, all must participate in "developing institutions and organizations that would intentionally counter the larger society's ideology about African Americans" (Perry, Steele, & Hilliard, 2003, p. 88) and all other marginalized people.

Oddly enough, civic culture, the social context within which we live our lives, while vital to the functioning of the society, isn't taught in school. But, in part, it's learned there; it's certainly experienced there. "It is transmitted by a complex process that includes training in many social institutions: family, peers, school, work, and the political system itself" (Almond & Verba, 1989, p. 498). Socialization into the civic culture, therefore, occurs through the direct exposure and interaction with the civic culture—the democratic polity—itself.

Democracy. John Dewey (1919/1966) and Gert Biesta (2007) both teach that democracy is not merely a mode of government but must also be understood as a "mode of 'associated living' characterized by inclusive ways of social and political action . . . [many] think of education as the *preparation* of children for their future participation in democratic life through the cultivation of a particular set of knowledge, values, and dispositions. . . . Some argue that democracy should simply be taught, while others maintain that the best way to create the democratic person is through participation in democratic structures and processes" (Biesta, 2007, p. 2; Dewey, 1919/1966; Westheimer & Kahne, 2004).

This means that the education we're after not only requires "all of us together," but also requires that there be ongoing processes through which nontraditional or previously excluded groups in a society are incorporated into the democratic mainstream. Di Palma (1990) shows that there must be some kind of inclusive and mutual agreement about who is a full member of the expanded group. He points out that "just as it takes time to craft an agreement, so it takes time and habituation before the agreement is secure and any danger of failure, stemming from the transition or its antecedents, is removed" (p. 110).

But agreements are crafted together and learned together with other insiders. People have to know that they belong, that they have full membership, in order to be in on the agreement. Thea Skocpol (1999) shows the historical importance of acknowledging the role of membership in large voluntary federations in forming individuals' understanding the rules and process of civic culture in general and in exercising their own power in particular. "People could be part of something immediate—with fellow locals they knew day to day—and part of grander endeavors at the same time" (p. 6).

Consequently, as we said at the beginning of this chapter, when the complexity and power of membership in multiple groups is rendered invisible by stereotypes, even the power and choices that those being marginalized do have are rendered invisible to the majority, precluding informed discourse. We saw consequences of that stereotyping when we met Franklin Johnstone. No discourse was possible during his undergraduate years—certainly not between him and his fellow students, and pretty soon, not even between Franklin and his long-standing ATDP associates. The culture of his university supported his being reduced to a stereotype and overlooked as a scholar, as a person. He didn't fit their stereotype, as he was also a member of a civic culture that, while still not ideal, was far more inclusive. Their frame of reference, inflexibly limited by stereotype, could not be made congruent with Franklin Johnstone's understanding of himself and of his scholarly performance.

In other words, understanding can't develop from outside of the actual arenas; inclusion and participation can't happen in theory, only in 3-space and real time. And, in our conversation, none of this can happen while many "students' political and social imaginations are circumscribed" (Perlstein, 2004, p. 1) by lack of full participation, as when marginalized groups of people are excluded from the group of the whole.

Well, that doesn't bode well for catchy things like "interventions" or playing "catch-up ball," but it does disclose why teaching "pages 6 through 10" doesn't close achievement gaps or increase equity in the society.

Daniel Perlstein focuses our discussion onto what does increase equity by acknowledging that all students benefit from peer effects within an ATDP kind of community of practice:

> Poor minority youth are in particular need of support and guidance to join the community of scholars, *but all youth need such support and guidance.* Because this is so, one can piggyback the interests of the marginalized on those of all. The poor benefit more than the rich from Social Security, but because all benefit, it is easier to get wide support for Social Security. There is more political muscle in its defense and the quality of the services is likely to be better. Just as Social Security both has a political constituency that welfare programs targeting the poor lack and will frequently be less brutalizing on it constituents, ATDP can serve marginalized students in ways that would be more difficult for Upwardbound and AVID. Peer effect matters. For policy makers it is worth spelling it out. (D. Perlstein, personal communication, February 18, 2004)

We hope that here, and in the two chapters that follow, we do just that.

Communities of practice reinforce civic culture. The importance of the community of practice, such as an ATDP or a multitude of others, is that it contains within it all of the knowledge required for becoming a functioning member of that community. Parameters exist around language used, complexity of thinking, rules by which members abide, and lots and lots of opportunities to practice and perform (Tusting, 2005). ATDP is an example of the novice-to-expert model that is voluntarily entered by a novice and through which the novice is directed and guided by the expert and supported by peers.

Please consider how very different the notions of support within a community of practice are from the commonly held notion of peer support and peer effects that states, "Jocelyn, Tanya, and Erika will benefit from being in class with high-performing students because they'll learn how to become more like the high performers." It's so different that it's reasonable to expect that Jocelyn's, Tanya's, and Erika's experiences will activate

stereotypes held by the high-performing students of the lower performing students, and that stereotype threats (McKown & Weinstein, 2003,
pp. 498–515) will be the product of the experience.

Within a community of practice everyone is there to gain the same
thing—expertise that is developed through purposeful work and sustained
effort under the guidance and encouragement of the expert. The momentum that builds within a community of practice gets its power from the
strength of the intellectual challenges facing all of the students. The students must rely on one another for social support—error checking, error
correction, and lots of encouragement. An expert, or someone farther along
the path to becoming one, models all of these things, and in turn, all of these
things are built into the structure of that community of practice. This is
about as far away from "go sit with Mildred because she's smart" as we
are from the former planet known as Pluto. It's whole galaxies away from
"signed, sealed, and delivered to the school door fully developed and
knowing everything already" and from the assumptions about students
and schools that support such statements.

From Novice to Expert Within a Community of Practice

Within communities of practice, skill development means something very
different from what is conventionally meant by these terms in schools and
classrooms. In contrast to the "drill-and-kill" connotation it frequently
carries, here it is based on a novice-to-expert way of thinking about purposeful learning. Berkeley philosophy professor Hubert Dreyfus's (1985)
model of skill acquisition begins with an uninitiated novice who has no
discretionary judgment about the area of activity and needs to adhere rig-
idly to rules and is at this point far more interested in accomplishing a goal
than in learning the rules. A novice, for example, who wants to become a
chef is far more interested in presenting an impressive dinner than in learning the chemistry that goes into the emulsification he's attempting or in
the knife work required to prepare salmon for sushi.

The remaining four stages on the road to expertise take one from being
able to use guidelines, while still lacking a holistic understanding, to ten-
tatively starting tasks on one's own (advanced beginner); to being able to
troubleshoot and know when to ask for help and beginning to see long-
term plans and goals (competent); to making self-corrections based on
previous learning, learning from the experience of others, and becoming
frustrated by the oversimplifications presented by others (proficient); all
the way to becoming an expert oneself and having enough information,
experience, and analytical abilities to rely on them instead of being bound
by rules (Daley, 1998; Dreyfus and Dreyfus, 1985; McClure, 2005; Prince &

Hoyt, 2002). Note how everyone has an affirmative status, every step of the way. Note that everyone is a full member of the group and is supported in exercising that membership.

In the novice-to-expert model exercised in a community of practice such as ATDP, we are removed entirely from the deficit model, full of its idea that "you should already know that." Rather, we're in an environment with plenty of room for "not knowing." We're in an environment where a premium is placed on learning to do. Within a community of practice the purpose is made clear, reinforced through work, and there is an anticipated outcome firmly in place (Wenger, McDermott, & Snyder, 2002). Therefore, the not-knowing-at-all of the greenest novice is ascribed a status that is very different from the kid in the corner of the classroom who is told to sit there until he has memorized a particular set of facts not clearly related to anything that anyone would ever wish to be good at. In contrast to that kid in the corner of the classroom, ATDP novices are within and bolstered by a community of practice.

ATDP students inhabit a rich environment, where they meet and work with students at all levels of learning, all having an expert to guide and direct them toward their own goal of becoming an expert. While the novice doesn't yet know exactly what the next steps will be, it is explicitly shown that every rule to be acquired will, when mastered, lead to the exercise of an anticipated skill and a step forward toward one's goal. All along the path, there will always be plenty of room for anticipatory socialization, and peer effects in this context have particular meaning and function in the making of an expert.

What does all of this look like in action? Can the elements of our discussion be put into practice within a summer program, a classroom, or a school before they operate within American society? Looking forward to Chapters 5 and 6, we will model and explore these elements of our discussion as they function at ATDP. Our hope is that ATDP's actions, interpretations, and stated beliefs will be convincing enough to provide policy makers, educators, parents, and community members with the support they need to bring academic talent development possibilities to the fore and available for all.

CHAPTER FIVE

Changing College-Going from Chance to Choice

SOME READERS MAY WONDER why we would devote an entire chapter to the subject of going to college. Is there a child in America who does not know about colleges and universities, who cannot rattle off the names of at least a half dozen schools of higher education? Have not the T-shirts and sweatshirts with university names and logos found their way to virtually every nook and cranny in our country, even those locations that cannot easily be reached by television stations showing college sports teams in action almost all year long?

The short answer is that in some respects, of course, college is very visible today. It would be hard to be an American and not know something about college as an official, widespread educational institution for youth between the ages of, say, 18 and 25. Elementary-school-aged children who do not know the name of their own state capital, who do not know that high schools have course and credit requirements for graduation, who perhaps do not know even what their mother or father does at work, nonetheless will tell you that it is very important to go to college. But what students know about college, how they think about their own college prospects, how likely they are to apply to college, how well-prepared they are to do so, and how likely they are to succeed in college, all depend a great deal on the homes children grow up in, the schools they attend, and the experiences of the adults and older youth who are integral parts of their lives.

IT STILL HELPS (A LOT) IF YOUR PARENTS ARE COLLEGE GRADS

By 1980, nearly 69% of the American population 25 years of age or older had completed at least 4 years of high school, and 17% of the same population had completed 4 or more years of college (U.S. Department of Education, 2003a, p. 17). And by 2001, the percentages had increased considerably: more than 84% of the American population 25 years of age or older had completed high school, and more than 26% of the same population had completed 4 or more years of postsecondary education (U.S. Department of Education, 2003a, p. 17).

A high school diploma now is an expected accomplishment (although not necessarily realized) for all American youth. A college education is becoming the presumed requirement for all who intend to make a living wage. But there are considerable inequities in who completes high school and who graduates from college.

Just Because People Assume Opportunities Exist, That Doesn't Mean They're Available

In 2001, while nearly 89% of White, non-Hispanic Americans 25 years of age or older had earned a high school diploma, the same was true for only 79.5% of Black Americans, and for only 56.5% of Hispanic Americans. The college degree statistics follow the same pattern: Although more than 28% of the White, non-Hispanic population 25 years of age or older had completed 4 or more years of college, the same could be said for only 16.1% of Black Americans and for only 11.2% of Hispanic Americans (U.S. Department of Education, 2003a, p. 17). And this gap cannot be closed if the pattern continues that White, non-Hispanic youth who complete high school are much more likely to be enrolled in college the following October than are Black or Hispanic high school completers (U.S. Department of Education, 2003b, p. 127).

The fact that Black and Hispanic adults are less likely to have completed college has significant consequences for secondary students. Policy Analysis for California Education (PACE) studies confirm this:

> Parents with no college education know less about academic preparation and college standards than college-educated parents. Consequently, students are less aware of postsecondary options, tuition costs, and required preparatory courses. (2004, p. 72)

U.S. Department of Education statistics further highlight the problem. Consider the statistics for high school completers who are then enrolled in college the following October. In 2001, more than 81% of high school completers whose parents had earned a bachelor's degree or higher were enrolled in college the following October. Only 51.9% of high school completers whose parents' highest educational attainment was a high school diploma or equivalent were enrolled in college. And only 39% of the high school completers whose parents had less than a high school diploma were enrolled in college (U.S. Department of Education, 2003b, p. 129).

College Must Be Made Visible Before It Can Be Made Available

Of course following in a parent's footsteps educationally, for better or worse, is not a new phenomenon. Even in Terman's *Genetic Studies of Genius*, high-IQ youth whose parents had not graduated from college were less likely to go to college themselves, or to graduate from college, than youth with similar high-IQ scores whose parents were college graduates (Getzels & Dillon, 1973, p. 697). There are undoubtedly many reasons why the academic experiences of parents may have trickle-down effects on their children.

PACE (2004) provides us with other data that make the case for the importance of ATDP efforts at making the university visible to children and youth. Currently, only about 35% of all California youth are proceeding from high school to college (p. 71). And although many California students aspire to attend college, they nonetheless demonstrate

> rather poor knowledge of college costs and policies. . . . Tuition was consistently overestimated, admission criteria were misunderstood, and students' knowledge of academic placement appeared to be based more on guesswork than fact. (p. 3)

Perhaps the most important finding presented in the PACE (2004) report is that many students among those proceeding from high school to postsecondary education simply are not clear "about what it takes to succeed in college" (p. 73). Knowing that one wants to go to college is quite different from knowing what college is about and knowing what will be required and expected. ATDP thus becomes a valuable source of information about access to and success in postsecondary education.

WE KNEW WE HAD TO GO TO COLLEGE; WE JUST DIDN'T KNOW WHAT COLLEGE WAS

When it comes to knowledge about college, therefore, even at the end of the first decade of the twenty-first century everyone is not equal in America. That alone makes it worth our close attention. For as common as talk about college might seem in America, many youth have little idea what would be involved in getting there, and then succeeding.

Mike Rose (1989) writes about this poignantly, from personal experience.

> I wasn't even aware of what "entrance requirements" were. My folks would say that they wanted me to go to college and be a doctor, but I don't know how seriously I ever took that; it seemed like a sweet thing to say, a bit of

supportive family chatter, like telling a gangly daughter she's graceful. The reality of higher education wasn't in my scheme of things. (pp. 34–35)

By the time Professor Rose wrote these lines in 1989, he had already been a professional educator for 2 decades, and it has now been a couple of decades since then. Yet for many, many youth, things haven't changed that much over time. Consequently, while making the university visible was and is nontrivial for anyone, it remains vital for many.

Wait a Minute! What Did You Say Grades Were For?

Not too many years ago, at a business-lunch meeting she conducted with two dozen ATDP students from low-performing, inner-city middle schools, the ATDP director was taken aback by a thoughtful and thought-provoking remark made by a student about to enter high school. The presenters at the meeting were three University of California outreach coordinators, themselves graduates of the middle schools represented. They were there to introduce the students to the importance of going to college (which it turned out each of the students could already state with appropriate stress and conviction) and to provide the students with a framework for preparing themselves to become competitive for college admission. Requirements? Prerequisites? Competitive? Now, that was a different story, it was a mystery.

Not one of the students present had knowledge of the course sequences they would need to take or of the level at which they would need to perform in order to make college attendance a possibility for them personally. That wasn't too surprising, as the students were still in middle school. They all nodded in agreement as information was distributed to them and was written on the chalkboard—they didn't know yet what any of it meant, but it looked like it might be something reasonable. However, when the presenters started talking about grades and the need to maintain a high grade point average, an eighth grader shot her hand into the air, "Wait, what do you mean about grades? What do grades mean? I'm going to college and I don't have those grades. What do grades have to do with going to college?" Her questions, from the looks on the faces of the students present, represented just what they were wondering. They were all certain that they were going to college. So, what did all of those other things have to do with college?

Building a Scheme of Things

ATDP takes seriously this need to introduce youth to the language, requirements and expectations of college—in other words, to build with them their own, well-informed, scheme of things. But the ATDP mission is different from the many programs that aim to help students, especially minority students, prepare to attend college (e.g., see the story of AVID reported in Mehan, Villanueva, Hubbard, & Lintz, 1996). The ATDP concern is not primarily with going to college, but rather with living an educated life. ATDP aims to help youth become competent and responsible scholars and consumers of knowledge, and in order to do that, college must be clearly visible.

This chapter, in fact, grew out of something Tomás Calderón, Coalinga Huron House alumnus (CHA House; Avenal was added to the name in 1999) and author of one of the ATDP college advice columns, had told to Nancy A. Mellor, the founder and director of CHA House (for more on Mellor, see Garrison, 2002). Calderón, presently a regional and city planner who specializes in public transit policy and works in Washington, D.C., had a pivotal conversation with Mellor as she prepared to earn her doctorate.

In preparation for her dissertation (adults connected with CHA House are wont to follow their students and go for more education; see Chapter 6), Mellor (2001) wanted to study hows and whys underlying the academic success of her students. As she was particularly interested in their college-going preparations and experiences, she set about conducting in-depth interviews with many who were already college graduates or currently in college.

The story Mellor anticipated she'd hear was that the alumni had never heard of college before they had met her; that it was she who had taught them about college, and then it was she who had sent them off to study. Mellor was taken aback by Calderón's reply, "Oh, no, Mrs. Mellor. We always knew that we were going to college. We just didn't know what college was. You taught us that. You and ATDP."

Calderón's close friend Robert Nobless, now a professor of political sociology and a doctoral graduate of Yale University, contributed some memories of one day while on the Berkeley campus for ATDP when he saw

> A short, wiry man with crazy hair, a disheveled look, old faded jeans, a T-shirt with [PHinisheD]. Like PhD. It was like, I'm doing the right thing. I'm going to be an academic. I always had a love affair with scholarship and knowledge and ideas, and Berkeley [ATDP] really fostered that and nurtured that . . . [and provided] certain key relationships, cushions actually. . . . It was coincidental that I ended up doing what I did. . . . I didn't know exactly what a PhD was; I knew that all those smart people have them and I'm smart. I want one. [That] was early in my life. (Mellor, 2001, p. 103)

As with Tomás Calderón, Robert Nobless knew early on that this was what he intended to do. He just didn't know what "this" might be. Left to chance, he might not have ever known it. But learning what college is and what an advanced degree is were things that he was eager to learn, and they were certainly ideas and lessons that he could be easily taught.

Clearly then, what students need is good, direct information to get them started on their journey. Yes, they certainly do.

Direct Information from Experts with Impressive School Ties

In June 2006 Robert's younger sister Marianne Nobless returned to the annual ATDP orientation meeting to speak to the audience of parents and students about her experiences as a former student. Now an advanced doctoral student in education policy, Marianne spoke about ATDP as "the reason behind my success."

Marianne was funny, poignant, and enthusiastic. She began by sharing something about her earliest years:

> I was born and raised in a small farming community in California's Central Valley. [To me, my town was] reminiscent of a Norman Rockwell painting. Small, friendly, and quaint. . . . my shelter from the outside world. We had no streetlights, two grocery stores, and everybody knew everybody.

Marianne came to ATDP for the first time when she was 12 years old. She was following in the footsteps of two older brothers who already had begun their own ATDP adventures, and was later followed by a sister. Marianne began her years at ATDP studying Writing and Latin, courses that would have greater influence on her life than she could have imagined at the time:

> I know, I know, Latin is a dead language. But that was the class I was determined to take. I felt super important walking around the campus practicing my conjugations in a language few other people understood. In later summers I went on to take Latin II and all the writing courses. . . . And that's it. We are products of our experiences. The classes I took at ATDP gave me a good foundation for all the academic challenges I later faced. . . . Four years later, as a sophomore in high school, I applied to a private Quaker school on the East Coast. The application consisted of two things: an essay and a standardized test. So I referred back to my writing classes for the writing component, and to my Latin classes for the vocabulary part of the standardized test.
>
> My courses at ATDP helped me not only in high school but they prepared me for college applications. They led me to Swarthmore as

an undergrad, and last year I returned to the first campus I had ever seen, right here at Berkeley, to begin my doctoral degree in education policy. . . . So to conclude, if you want your kids to be successful, they are on the right path because they are in ATDP. But if they are taking Latin or Writing they will be unstoppable.

She captivated parents and youth alike, especially when she told a funny story about a renowned ATDP Latin teacher. Soon after the group meeting ended, a line formed at the ATDP office with requests for last-minute admission into any space that might be available in the Latin classes.

Things to Think About as You Learn to Make Choices

Years earlier, toward the end of the summer of 1993, the ATDP newsletter included its first set of columns written by ATDP alumni (including one by Marianne's oldest brother Robert) about the colleges they had chosen for themselves and were currently attending. Five students cheerfully extolled the merits of their choices: MIT, St. Mary's College, Stanford, Oberlin, and Swarthmore. Each student responded to the same prompts: What are the basics about your college? What made it your choice? What are its greatest strengths? What are its drawbacks? To whom would you recommend it? When are you available to meet with [current ATDP] students who wish to learn more about your college?

These ATDP alumni with the very impressive school ties rightfully were proud of their transition from high school to college, and of the particular choices they made. Each told a different story, of course. But the set of stories definitely had a common theme—theirs was a college for students who were interested in being academically challenged. The students wrote about working "toward excellence," about an environment infused with "searching for one thing—knowledge," about "dedicated professors, rigorous courses," and about the great value that each college, and each student writing about the college, placed on education.

Of Course They Know; They're Experts

What is most striking about these statements, but mostly invisible, is that these columns were written by students who, but for the ATDP experience, might never have applied to the colleges they were then attending. These were students from, as one student labeled it, "a poor, rural, oil and farming community in the San Joaquin Valley." A college education was not a routine experience for the youth, or the adults, from this community. One student wrote in her column, "I am Mexican American and the first woman in my family to attend a 4-year postsecondary institution, the first to graduate from high school."

ATDP had helped make college visible, desirable, and accessible for these youth. ATDP had encouraged these students and their families to dream about possibilities associated with higher education; and the program had helped them learn, step-by-step, how to turn dreams into realities. Through their ATDP experiences, and supported by their peers and their middle school math teacher (now district superintendent) Nancy Mellor, students and families traveled a path from the fields to the academy. Because the students and families traveled together, over the past 2 decades they have stayed connected to hometown and, as Marianne put it, to "the outside world."

WHILE THINGS ARE GOOD FOR SOME AS IS, THEY DON'T IMPROVE ON THEIR OWN

Of course not all youth who take part in ATDP need the program to help them think about and plan for college. Some children know a great deal about college long before they even realize what they know. Some come to ATDP hoping the program will help them get into the college of their choice. Children who grow up in homes with parents who are college graduates and perhaps even hold graduate degrees, or in homes with older brothers and sisters who have joined the college-going nation, have a leg up on thinking about college, applying to college, even building their youthful lives in concert with where they think college may take them. For these students, ATDP serves partly as confirmation for how they have been preparing and planning and partly as one more voice identifying and emphasizing different aspects of going to college.

Recall the range of parent educational experience we spoke of earlier in this book (see Introduction; Chapters 1 and 3). Many ATDP students do not grow up in homes with parents who are college graduates or in homes where very specific talk about college begins early in a child's life. This is especially true for the students from ATDP cohorts in the Central Valley, to whom we've just referred, and from other areas throughout the Bay Area with low-performing schools and unschooled families.

For the students who grow up in homes where college has not already become part of the family experience, ATDP is an awakening to both expectations and possibilities. These youth see, hear about, and live, perhaps for the first time, the life of college. They learn the language of going to college, the requirements, and the road they might travel. They learn to live the experience, not just paying passing visits to view others living it—it's an inside-outside thing, and they learn from the inside.

A SENSE OF BELONGING AND AN ACTUAL PLACE TO BELONG

We have been talking about making clear the idea and process required to bring students to the university. We have seen that there is both directness and considerable subtlety in making the university visible to students. Let's also remember that the university is a real place, not just a wonderful but abstract idea. In making the university visible there is an element of merely having to look around, watch where one is walking, think for just one moment about where one is sitting. We will continue to discuss the subtlety shortly, but first let us acknowledge the elephant in the room: the Secondary Division for ATDP takes place on the UC Berkeley campus.

This campus typically is referred to either as "Cal" or "Berkeley." The sports teams are the "Cal" Bears, but "Berkeley" is home to Nobel laureates and serves as the URL introduction to the school. UC Berkeley is distinguished not only within the state of California but also across the country and the world. Its academic excellence is signaled by its faculty laureates, members of the National Academy of Sciences, members of the National Academy of Engineering, and, as its catalog notes, "more NSF Young Investigators than there are at any other university in the country." Many of Berkeley's academic departments and schools consistently rank among the top in the country. Berkeley is not only academically prestigious, it is also physically stunning. The catalog describes the setting this way: "Students study, work, and relax among Neoclassical buildings, wooden glens, and parklands spread across 1,232 scenic acres overlooking the San Francisco Bay." There is the requisite space on the campus for bands and speeches and protests: Berkeley's Sproul Plaza is known far beyond the campus and the state as the home of the Free Speech Movement in the 1960s. There are libraries all across the campus, large and small, focused and general, too many to count. There are hills and streams and sculpture on the grounds. The campus is stunning.

And, of course, the campus is surrounded by the city of Berkeley. The university catalog explains that Berkeley "has a long history as one of America's most lively, culturally diverse, and politically adventurous cities." These are gentle words for a city also known as the "People's Republic of Bezerkely," a slogan that can be found emblazoned on T-shirts worn by tourists and students alike.

It's a Nice Place to Visit, But Could I Ever Live Here?

We are making a big fuss about Berkeley being Berkeley because most people, for better or worse, have a strong image of it and can easily envision both students from within the culture of college-going families and students from far outside of it being invited to be a part of its life. But please treat it as a metaphor for all college and university campuses, all over the country. College is a magical place where wondrous things can happen and all students would benefit from ATDP-type experiences there.

At the same time that we assure you that the magical college experiences can and do happen everywhere, we remind you that it's also ordinary, and that's a good thing because it means that it can be made manageable. Regardless of students' backgrounds, they all climb the stairs of old and new buildings, learning to distinguish between the home of the physicists and the home of the paleontologists (which, by the way, is graced by the statue of a saber-toothed tiger—but then again, Valley Life Sciences has a whole dinosaur in its lobby). The university is their school for 6 weeks: its buildings, classrooms, equipment, libraries, pathways, and eating venues. Even the most jaded of the teenagers is likely to be impressed, at least privately.

By the end of even a single summer, however, the ATDP youth at Berkeley learn not to be impressed by most of the classrooms—they're just ordinary. Except for the laboratories, which are very well equipped, the classrooms tend to be filled with old, unmatched, and wobbly tables and chairs, or, worse, the old-style chair-table combination attached permanently to the floor. The youth also learn there is nothing particularly impressive about the food facilities on the Berkeley campus (standard pre-packaged or cafeteria fare), or about computer access (too many people, too few machines). But the whole is much greater than the sum of its parts. And after having spent purposeful time there, "students forever after will hold an image" (Boulding, 1961) of college as a place where they might walk regularly someday, and an image of a particular university against which they can compare and contrast other universities. Yet seeing and feeling the physical "place" are but a small part of developing an understanding of what it means to go to college and to make good use of the college experience.

RITUALS, TRADITIONS, AND SYMBOLS TO CONVEY THE SPIRIT AND PURPOSE OF ATDP

We agree strongly with Mike Rose's statement that there is nothing as exclusive as the academic club (see Chapter 2). From Rose's own experiences, perhaps from your own, and certainly from the experiences of those you know and from histories you've read, you know that memberships to the academic club are available and are a possibility. Our conversation takes that as a given. Our conversation, rather, is intended to present and underline ways of changing club membership for many from a chance occurrence into a deliberate choice. We've given examples of academic tracks that students have laid and traveled. We've also made reference to the social structures required for stability and sustainability of individuals who choose to join the club.

In *The Presentation of Self in Everyday Life* (1959), Erving Goffman shows how social transformations (in our story, from outsider to insider) are taught and learned:

> [When] the individual takes on a task that is not only new to him but also unestablished in the society, or if he attempts to change the light in which the task is viewed, he is likely to find that there are already several well-established fronts from among which he must choose. Thus, when a task is given a new front we seldom find that the front that is given is itself new. (p. 28)

So people who choose to join the academic club need to, can, and do learn how to make it known that they are members. They learn through experience and instruction. Goffman shows us how rituals practiced by the insiders provide some of the foremost instruction in teaching newly inducted insiders the nature and functions of their roles. He shows how individuals, by participating in the club's own rituals, learn how insiders think and feel, how they display who they are, how they express themselves, how they dress and behave, and how they display their pride in their own accomplishments. Goffman shows us how ritual conveys and perpetuates these roles.

For these reasons, ATDP takes its rituals and symbols seriously, weaving them through the students' and parents' experiences with the program. These symbols and rituals help to make

> history and tradition intrude at every turning, their message crystal clear. It says to students in particular that this institution has a noble past, and they are now a part of it. It says too that they have a vast community of supporters . . . who are and were proud of their connection with the school and who . . . would expect the same of those there today. (Jackson, 1981, p. 124)

ATDP makes use of long-standing rituals and symbols to define its mission to students, parents, and faculty in order to enlist their active participation in the community. The orientation meeting we have discussed is one of these rituals. There, returning students and their families come as much to renew their membership by hearing the latest student stories, meeting old-timers, and welcoming newcomers (students and teachers alike), as much as they come to take care of their own course-specific business. The student and occasional parent speakers do more to build a community with a common vision than could ever be realized merely by answering student and parent questions individually. This conversation group places the new individuals and their questions into a welcoming, inclusive, community context.

When a parent who spoke in 2004 told the story of her worries the first time she'd sent her son off to ("the weird planet") Berkeley for the summer, she clearly touched the hearts and minds of many parents new to the program. Adults gathered around her afterward to chat, offer words of thanks, and ask their own questions. The group chatted for quite a while.

The program catalog, the Saturday orientation, and the welcome letters the teachers write to students, are "opening notes" that define what it means to be an ATDP student. Like the "da da da dum" of Beethoven's Fifth Symphony, these symbols and rituals announce the program. They help to set a tone. The message the program aims to convey is that this will be different from students' other schooling experiences elsewhere. This is an introduction to the life of the Academy. This program is purposeful, professional, passionate, and disciplined, and it calls upon students to be the same. ATDP uses traditions and rituals to convey its purpose and to carry the process forward and sees them as a vital part of changing "chance" to "choice." As in other social organizations the rituals and traditions link members together and provide added momentum to the whole group.

LEARNING THE STEPS THAT CHANGE CHANCE TO CHOICE

When students apply to ATDP they learn how to apply to college. They must examine the program catalog carefully and decide which course of study might best meet their needs and interests—and even make sure that they have the prerequisites for a particular class. They must gather a variety of information about themselves, which involves thinking about work they have done that speaks well to their academic competence and interests, and also soliciting the assistance of teachers who can speak to their abilities and attitudes. Then they must make their best case for why they should be accepted by the program. To be students in ATDP they must take note of the commitments they are making to serious work and the life of the mind, and actually sign on to making these commitments.

University life begins and ends with serious academic work. It comes quickly and intensely. The ATDP catalog, orientation, and welcoming notes from teachers with the students' first assignments signal students that they will be expected to do much work and the pace will be rapid. The symbols and rituals also try to make clear that this is a community with considerable support if a student seeks it out and chooses to make use of it. The symbols and rituals make all participants aware that *we* are all part of ATDP—there's no *they*. A weekly newsletter, a summer-end poster session, and an annual after-program picnic bring together students taking courses in classrooms all across the Berkeley campus, along with their families and former students. And now, class Web pages along with students' online discussions serve to tie program members closer and extend their interests farther.

The weekly newsletter that ATDP produces during the 6-week program is filled with information from across the program and provides an important medium for communication across classes. It reminds everyone that they are part of something larger than their own class. Some information is UC Berkeley specific: about the libraries, including their hours, their rules, the various online catalogs, and the best place to catch a snooze; about the Language Center and the Computer Lab; about the shuttle bus that "makes the perimeter of campus every eight to ten minutes [and] now costs $1." Students are thanked by the director for teaching her that "Haas now [also] refers to the Haas Pavilion (formerly Harmon Gym) on Bancroft Way and not only to the Haas School of Business," and are reminded to "smell the roses" at the UC Berkeley Botanical Gardens and visit the pterosaur in the lobby of the Life Sciences. A box on the cover of the newsletter proclaims:

> Here you will find program news and announcements and learn about what is happening in different ATDP classes. . . . [The newsletter] is also about you: We provide a forum through which you can share your thoughts and work. Submit your poetry, editorials, reviews, photographs, or pieces of art to the Editors at the ATDP office.

There is always a column "From the Director":

> You know that you are here to learn, to grow, to work, and you can be sure that you will. But it is important that you not engage in your pursuits alone. You are also here to be an active part of a community dedicated to learning and to intellectual and social growth. So, offer your hand in friendship to others in your class, and accept theirs when it is extended to you.

Generally, there are pictures: the office staff; students' entries for a photo contest; snapshots from classes in action; pictures from ATDP "long, long ago"; and pictures from around the campus. These campus pictures sometimes are part of the weekly ATDP Challenge ("a weekly opportunity for you to exercise your mind, stretch your legs, and win fabulous prizes [maybe even a T-shirt!]" For example, one challenge was given as this: "Only one edifice on the campus has a Latin inscription. Where is the inscription and what does it say?" Another challenge sent students on hunts for special places on the campus, submitting photos of themselves at each place. The winner, photographed by friends, was shown with his head in the mouth of one bear statue on the campus and being given a bear hug by an even larger statue. Keep in mind that the task of matching building names and statues to the pictures taken of them or near them is not easy for anyone, even tenured faculty, on this campus of 1,232 acres.

Other times students are invited to take part in recreational sports on campus or to attend events. The newsletter also carries interviews with students who have come from places like Russia or China to stay with relatives and attend the program. The newsletter also offers information for students thinking beyond the ATDP program in other ways.

The last issue for the summer of 2007 was extra long. It contained photographs of student work from folk art bear masks to self-portraits, to groups of students sketching their ideas. The issue listed the titles of some important pieces of work produced by students that summer: An eighth grader's research paper, "Poverty in Early America"; a Folk Art and Literature student's self-illustrated study of "Powerful Women, from Ruth Asawa to Our Lady of Guadalupe"; a paper written by a ninth grader titled "Eulogies for the Fallen: Protagonists and Antagonists in *Heart of Darkness* and in *Harry Potter and the Half-Blood Prince*"; and a group of AP Psychology students' research report, "Does Rejection Hurt? An fMRI Study of Social Exclusion."

The final issue also promised,

> You will also read about a group of young intellectuals whose core group are ATDP students, whose imaginations and visions have been fired by the passionate need to know about their world and the life of the mind.

The group had named itself The Young Thinkers' Society, forming after several students did not want to end the discussions they had begun in their philosophy class. They submitted an excerpt of their mission statement for publication in the final issue of the newsletter:

> Our mission is to promote the intellectual development of young individuals for life. . . . [O]ur vision: To create an intellectual community of young individuals in which ideas are openly shared and discussed. . . . Central to the way the Young Thinkers' Society

carries out its mission is [through] free peer discussion, unsuper-
vised by adults. . . . Moreover, [we believe that through serious
discussions] the individual is made outward-looking, and through
tackling the same questions as those tackled by the philosophers
and sages of today and yesterday, the young individual may even
make a difference in solving such fascinating problems.

RITUALS AND TRADITIONS FOR TEACHERS
WHO PLAY EXPANDED ROLES

During the year a very large portion of the ATDP faculty teach in public
K–12 schools, but in our experience the ATDP culture is markedly different than that ordinarily experienced by public school teachers. To mark
the differences, ATDP promotes symbols, traditions, and rituals that support faculty in thinking of themselves and their profession in expanded,
far more collegial ways. Because the course descriptions and syllabi are
identified as "belonging" to the teachers who create them, both general
faculty and department-specific meetings center on the faculty's thoughts
and questions.

Department meetings frequently last far beyond the appointed hour,
as teachers take or even grab the opportunity to conduct very animated
and social conversations about the disciplines for which they share a common passion. Gratifying exchanges take place between "old hands" in the
teaching business and brand-new teachers, one group enthusiastically
bringing the wisdom that comes over time and the other bringing new technologies and thinking—but sometimes it's the old guard bringing new technologies and novices bringing wise views and recommendations.

Ownership of Intellectual Products; Import of Teachers' Work

The teachers' own course binders form the documents of record for the
program and for themselves. The binders for every course ever taught as
part of the program are maintained. These binders are added to or recon-
structed each year, but the history of the course always is left intact. The
binders make it relatively easy for teachers to do the business of the program: There are sections for the program attendance sheets, emergency
information forms, field trip permission forms, homework referral forms,
and class record sheets for student work from each session.

The most important sections of the binder, though, are the lesson plan
summaries the teachers are asked to prepare for each class (the form asks
for objectives, plan for use of class time, assignments, and the teacher's own

reflections on the lesson) and copies of all the materials the teacher distributes to the students during the summer session.

New teachers to the program automatically are given past years' binders to look through as they prepare their own courses, and returning teachers receive their past years' binders at the first preprogram meeting. These are not merely casual references for the teachers and program staff; they represent the historical record of curriculum, instruction, and assessment for the life of the program. They underline that learning and improvement are important and ongoing,

The teacher binders have even taken on a life outside the program. A faculty member at UC Berkeley played a lead role in developing the standardized mathematics readiness tests used across the state of California. Subsequently, when he was called on to teach teachers and mathematics specialists what an ideal Algebra I program might look like on a lesson-by-lesson basis, he called the ATDP program director and asked to borrow the set of Algebra I binders from the program, which had been developed by the longtime course instructor. They were lent only with permission from the teacher who had created them—permission both for who was to use them, how they would be used, and how her work was to be credited.

Teachers' Experiences Widely Heard and Heeded

One year the chair of the science department wrote in the newsletter about opportunities that ATDP provides for teachers: "the intellectual stimulus of working with motivated, bright students . . . [as well as] the chance to get my 'thinking batteries' recharged." She went on in her short statement to talk as a teacher at college might about a favorite seminar:

> I wish we could call it ATP rather than ATDP, because ATP is the universal energy currency of living things and energy is something all Program students develop as the summer progresses.

More than a decade later, two doctoral students who teach in the psychology department of the University of California at Davis proposed to team-teach an ATDP class. They wrote of their experiences and reflections for the final issue of the 2007 newsletter:

> Teaching the AP Psychology course was our first true collaborative teaching effort and our first experience with ATDP. Simply put, it has been wonderful! So far, our classroom and the program has exceeded our expectations in nearly every way and we hope to continue with it for as many years as we can.

There is such a fluid interaction among those who work for ATDP, that even daunting tasks are (nearly) painless and *always* forward-looking. We try to emulate this fluid interaction in our daily cooperative teaching and class preparation. This positive attitude toward education is the main attribute of the ATDP program we've noticed, and we attempt to bring into our classroom and develop in our students.

The most rewarding experience for us came during the end of one of our classes where we brought in Berkeley graduate students in Developmental Psychology to talk to the students about their research. We spent some time talking with our students about life both during and after college: This included the "Big" question of "What am I going to do when I grow up?" One thing we told them was that life was going to be difficult because it's going to require hard work and long hours. That's just something most people won't be able to change. One aspect about life that can be under the student's control is the interest level that they have in whatever career they decide to follow. Don't follow the money, just simply follow your best dreams and the rest will come with hard work.

We can confidently say that we love what we are doing at ATDP. Although the work was hard and challenging, we loved helping and witnessing our students learn. This is more than enough motivation for us to go about our job with the zest that we do. It's our hope that our students see and emulate this passion to spark a career that will enable them to live out their own dreams.

IT'S MORE THAN AN IMAGE OF COLLEGE; IT'S A WAY OF CONDUCTING BUSINESS

Efforts to make university life pervasive begin with the ATDP catalog. The catalog opens with a letter from the program director, a statement of purpose about the program, and an invitation to the reader to join in this mission. The program catalog then continues with more information of the sort you would expect to find in any college catalog: information about the faculty, the campus, admissions, fees and tuition, important dates, and so on. Course descriptions are arranged by departments. Each class indicates faculty name and class days and times. Classes are scheduled either 2 or 3 days a week, depending on the number of credits attached to the course, with each class session lasting 3½ hours. In other words, the ATDP catalog speaks the language of college.

Setting Up Shop

Everything about first encounters with the program, beginning with the catalog and the process of applying, aims to signal that this is different from K–12 education. Students are reminded that they are making a choice to attend ATDP, and that they must make a choice, also, about what to study. In turn, because they have so chosen, the program expects them to want to learn, to come with their own motivation. The program will provide intellectual and material resources; students must be willing to put in the requisite sweat equity. Just like college.

The ATDP catalog includes at its center a four-page application. The application process, as we discussed earlier, closely resembles the process of applying to college. Here potential students must select one course for the summer, akin to selecting a college major, from the catalog outline of courses within departments. Potential students are required to submit a teacher recommendation, their most recent grades, and their scores from the most recent standardized achievement test they have taken. The youth are required to outline their interests and activities in and outside of school. Finally, they are required to submit a piece of work they have completed in the past school year, or write a well-developed essay of no more than 1,500 words on one of two topics provided.

The acceptance packet includes information about the books that will be used in the course and where to buy them. Generally, buying books is not a K–12 public school experience. For elementary and secondary students, books typically are distributed in class by the teacher and returned to the teacher at the end of a semester or a school year. But of course that is not how college works, and neither is it how ATDP works. ATDP students go to the same bookstore that Berkeley college students visit to purchase books. And the ATDP books are presented in the same book sections, in the same manner, as are books for any college class.

This Business Needs to Be Funded

Again, unlike K–12 public schooling, college needs to be funded. For some, this will never pose a problem; for others, this is a barrier. So there is a financial aid section to the application, a signal that this also is something to be aware of when applying to college. ATDP offers financial aid to approximately a quarter of its students. Families must send a copy of their income tax forms with all the schedules and must complete a questionnaire assessing financial need. Full subsidies are given to families living below the poverty line. If ATDP staff are not sure how to handle a particular case, they turn to the UC Berkeley financial aid office, which has considerable expertise in this area, to assist with the decision.

Well, That's Interesting, but What About College?

Of course all ATDP youth will not assimilate the theory and practice of college through the work they do and the ways they work in classes. For some, those messages are far too subtle. ATDP has other ways of communicating the more practical messages about college and, especially, about preparing for college.

One way of communicating things directly is to just tell the story, and that's what ATDP does when it invites admissions officers from the different colleges that comprise what students think of as Berkeley. Parents are invited to attend. Presenters share a great deal of practical information, including steps to take in preparation for college, and where to find little-known but readily available information about such topics as special programs and financial aid. Most important, admissions officers ask students and their parents to please not focus their college planning on what they think will look good on a résumé, but instead to focus on developing authentic academic interests and finding their own passions. Many learn an important lesson when they hear the presenter say, "We're especially interested in seeing what you have done with the opportunities available to you. We want to know what you hope to gain from attending this university and what you can contribute to it." Messages like that help make the university more visible to many.

Even in the smallest ways, the idea of college, including the intellectual idea, is communicated again and again. ATDP students learn a great deal about the subject they study for the summer. They also learn a great deal about college. They learn what it looks like and feels like. They learn what they have to do to be admitted. They learn about the opportunities and expectations they will encounter when they enroll. Sociologists and psychologists might label this a period of *anticipatory socialization*, learning how to perform in a role that we aspire to but do not yet occupy (e.g., see Merton, 1957; Getzels, 1963). And as we saw from the discussion of anticipatory socialization in Chapter 3, it not only sparks the imagination of the young and not so young, it makes being a novice a worthwhile thing and permits trying on the mantle of an expert.

ATDP IS LIKE COLLEGE, EXCEPT WHEN IT'S NOT

There is one significant way in which ATDP differs—intentionally—from the college experience: The program works seriously to build in supports that will encourage student success. Especially because coursework is difficult and the pace is relentless, ATDP tries to keep students from getting lost or falling behind. The support systems ATDP has built over the years aim not only to help students do competent work under intense situations, but also to teach students when and how to seek out help for themselves.

Support begins within courses. As we have noted already, students receive their teacher's e-mail address, telephone number, and "hotline" hours, and the teacher will ask that every student call at least once, early in the course, if only just to say hello. The aim is to help students learn to initiate student-teacher conversations.

These individual conversations and whole-group ones in class establish and reiterate ATDP's approach to learning. On the first day of class every student is given a list of names and phone numbers for all students in their class. The class list and the first week's newsletter are intended to help build community and help students think about their classmates and others in the program as sources of academic support. So, for example, this conversation took place on the first day of class in one AP Biology class. Describing her expectations for the class, the teacher said: "I'd like to encourage you to work together. What I want you to feel really comfortable about is working together. How many of you do that already, share?" Only about three students raised their hands. The teacher acknowledged, "Most of the time that isn't encouraged in school." A student called out, spontaneously, "That's cheating." But working together is not cheating in ATDP, as the teacher emphasized to the students: "ATDP really encourages that. That's why you've got the list of phone numbers."

The pedagogy of ATDP classes encourages learning with classmates. Students routinely work in pairs or in small groups. They learn to examine and critique the work of others. They learn to take advantage of the expertise of others in the service of their own learning. They learn that the knowledge of the group truly is greater than the knowledge of any individual.

The fact that ATDP is organized like a college experience, with students attending class just two or three times a week (depending on the number of credits assigned to the course) and being expected to do a great deal of work outside of class, sometimes is problematic for these middle school and high school students. ATDP is prepared for this. As a start, ATDP teachers are asked to keep careful watch on student progress and are provided the support needed to do so. From the very first time a student shows significant difficulty with a concept or task, the teacher and a program academic counselor follow up with the student.

ATDP's head counselor, Professor Beverly Vandiver, teaches individual students how to become active learners in their particular class. The service is a vital one across the program for all students, both the ones who are always at the top of their class in school and have never had to study actively in order to remain there, and the ones from classrooms where too little challenge is presented to students.

Support at ATDP extends outside each classroom. Each ATDP department offers one-on-one tutoring sessions, and the program as a whole offers subject-specific learning labs. The tutoring and the labs have taken very definite forms over time and there is a particular lore that has grown around them. For example, some without an ATDP frame of mind predicted that the labs and obvious tutoring might draw a distinction between students who need help and those who don't.

Those who know ATDP can easily guess what the students' actual response to the labs and tutoring would be. As one student wrote in his evaluation of his lab, "This is just great. I never got to ask as many questions as I want to before. No one tells me to let someone else have a chance. There's plenty of time for all of us." The most frequently asked question about the one-on-one tutoring is, "Can I sign up for two sessions in a row?" Our personal favorite question about tutoring was asked by a student from a low-performing high school who was enrolled in AP Biology at the time: "I know that I'm not in a math class, but could I please sign up for math tutoring? I have some questions from my math class last year that I couldn't get answered, and I *really* want to know."

One-on-one tutoring is free, and students may avail themselves of this support as much or as little as they choose. A student must sign up for a tutoring session in advance, and at the start of a tutoring session, the student must articulate the question(s) he or she wants to address. No one can come to a tutoring session and merely state: "I don't get it." Students are expected to figure out—often with a teacher's assistance or a peer's assistance—what they want help with. Students learn quickly that they can't get their work done for them, but they can learn how to work with the ideas and the assignments for their course.

Broader summer-long help comes in the form of learning labs that students sign up for in parallel with specific courses. These labs are intended to provide structure and academic support for students who think they might benefit from additional assistance. The labs also are designed to teach students "what they don't teach you in school about learning," as the ATDP director frequently puts it. The instructors work closely with classroom teachers on key concepts of the course and their applications; some of the lab instructors are UC Berkeley students earning teaching credentials, others are credentialed teachers who want to learn more about learning.

Everyone connected with ATDP frequently reminds anyone who will listen that all of us together really are smarter than any one of us alone, and that all of us need to be academically nurtured and mentored—some at home, some elsewhere. ATDP's learning labs teach about the work that typically goes on behind the scenes in homes with well-educated parents: the practice and rehearsal that takes place before class, frequently with parents helping and/or debriefing students afterward. The mentor tutor labs provide a designated occasion for rehearsing how a concept might be explained, how it might be visible in different contexts, how it might be applied, and so on. The lab instructor helps break down classwork, demonstrating how any given session is connected to what has happened before and anticipate what might be coming up shortly.

The group might brainstorm papers or homework assignments before sending students off to do the actual work at home. Some lab instructors are known for taking their tutees to campus coffee houses where they discuss readings and examine course assignments, as well as look around and feel what it would be like to be a college student. Whether the sessions are held in coffee houses or in classrooms, their regular nature and the intensity of the work for the group often help the students become part of a tight-knit friendship group of learners.

ATDP students may again participate in the journey from novice to expert, as many of the ATDP courses also have teaching assistants: youth who have completed the class a year or so earlier and are helping in class now in a paraprofessional way. They work under the direction of the classroom teacher and sometimes have their own telephone hours also. All teaching assistants are paid; those interested are entitled to a free course in the program. Teaching assistants help during class sessions as appropriate; they model conversation; they serve as just slightly older and more experienced peers who help students in the class reach one step higher than their current knowledge and skill. For example, on the first day of an AP Biology course the teaching assistant (formerly a student in this same course) introduced himself as a new high school graduate, headed to Stanford, intending to major in molecular biology and minor in political science. This personal biography clearly grabbed the students' attention. The teaching assistant added, about the course and the program: "It's really a fun time. Get to know different kids. Meet people and have fun and learn while you're at it."

In all of these ways and many more, ATDP students are encouraged to engage in personal contacts in the service of developing academic expertise and learning to be successful in college. The students learn to talk with teachers by having substantive conversations on topics of mutual interest. They learn to work with peers on consequential assignments that do, indeed, benefit from the wisdom of more than one person. They learn to look to slightly older youth as guides and models. The social influences of ATDP are wide and deep, carefully thought out in some ways, and haphazardly fortunate in others.

IT'S NOT JUST A SENSE OF PLACE; IT'S A SENSE OF MY PLACE

There is considerable good will associated with this venture, turning what some see as a cold ivory tower or hot bed of radicalism into a warm and delightful place to send their children. Parents love being on campus, and they love having their children on the campus. Families from widely different communities especially appreciate the opportunity for their children to come to know the variety of ATDP students, expanding access to people different from those in their home communities and breaking down stereotypes. Students return to their middle schools and high schools and speak favorably about the campus and knowledgeably about how to plan for college. And finally, in the list of the benefits the university accrues from this program, ATDP prepares students for and recruits students into undergraduate programs at Berkeley. In fact, a significant number of Berkeley Incentive Award winners—recipients of a competitive scholarship program for students who have overcome the greatest odds and have shown great academic progress—have been ATDP students.

College is many things. It is, today, the minimum requirement for youth hoping to earn a living wage during their adulthood. It is an opportunity to meet people from beyond one's immediate neighborhood and to learn about lives lived by others in our large and diverse country. It is also "school" with lofty goals:

> transmitting the intellectual heritage of . . . civilization; fostering a high level of verbal and mathematical skills; developing an in-depth understanding of social, cultural, and political institutions; facilitating one's ability to think reflectively, analytically, critically, synthetically, and evaluatively; developing one's value structures and moral sensibilities; facilitating personal growth and self-identity; and fostering one's sense of career identity and vocational competence. (Pascarella & Terenzini, 1991, p. 1)

Universities also are communities of scholars. They are places inhabited by people whose lives are entwined around learning, teaching, and advancing knowledge. ATDP invites youth to begin to think about whether they, too, might want to live intellectual lives.

ATDP students spend their summer engaged in tasks and using tools that are natural, ongoing, and valued in academic communities and represent the work of the community. Students publish poetry books, short stories, and research abstracts. They build architectural and engineering models. They read and then perform Shakespeare. They spend hours using the very same equipment in laboratories that professional scientists use (and the ATDP students sign off on strict rules for work in those labs). They work with library collections that are important to university scholars.

ATDP students get a 6-week glimpse of the life of a university and life at a university.

Perhaps the most critical part of the invitation ATDP makes to the youth of the program is the chance to spend time with people who live their lives as members of the academic community. Youth have the opportunity to come to know these people—their teachers, teaching assistants, mentor tutors, program support staff—and think about how they feel in the company of these people.

We hope the students are living a version of Mike Rose's (1989) experience:

> My teachers modeled critical inquiry and linguistic precision and grace, and they provided various cognitive maps for philosophy and history and literature. They encouraged me to make connections and to enter into conversations—present and past—to see what talking a particular kind of talk would enable me to do. . . . And it was all alive. . . . They liked books and ideas, and they liked to talk about them in ways that fostered growth rather than established dominance. They lived their knowledge. And maybe because of that their knowledge grew in me in ways that led back out to the world. I was developing a set of tools with which to shape a life. (p. 58)

The ATDP community—including the adults and the groups of youth in classes across the Berkeley campus—aims to help shape and inspire life's possibilities. Youth are offered models for their own futures. They are offered resources in support of developing knowledge and skill. They learn standards for work—for work by the novice, the knowledgeable layman, and the expert. Youth are offered many and varied opportunities to see themselves as members of the academic community, to come to know the commitments, and to watch and live out for themselves the process of a community at work and always renewing itself.

ATDP invites a diverse student population, partnering with programs such as UC Berkeley's Early Academic Outreach Program (EAOP), districts such as Reef-Sunset and West Contra Costa Unified School Districts, and many individual members of school faculties, to invite to ATDP low-income and first-in-the-family college-prep students they work with. These programs, districts, and classrooms are in areas not reached by ATDP's tiny staff. Thus their collaboration greatly increases ways of entrance into the academic community and helps make membership a matter of choice rather than chance.

Where and to whom the youth were born suddenly becomes much less important than usual in academic and career choices. Instead, what matters more is whether youth are able to find a fit between their own interests and inclinations and the possibilities that are available to them in colleges and universities. What does it mean to find a fit between one's own interests and inclinations and the possibilities available in colleges and universities? Would ATDP be satisfied only if a significant number of its alumni went on to careers as scientists and scholars? Is academic talent development served only by these ends? Our answer, as you surely suspect, is: "No, of course not. The development of academic talent covers a range of achievements and a continuum of accomplishment." What this continuum looks like, and how ATDP contributes to movement along it, will be taken up in Chapter 6.

The Gift of Community and the Community of Gifts

IN THIS CHAPTER WE TELL many stories, mixing accounts of personal experiences with descriptive statistics about the many students who have passed through ATDP classes but have remained part of the ATDP community into adulthood. We write about what students say about the program and what they do with their lives after they have completed their participation. We give voice to what students have told us about their classes, their teachers, and their fellow students. In various ways we try to communicate the difference the program has made (and has not made) in the lives of students it has served. And parents speak, too.

We offer these stories to show that communities of practice and academically rich neighborhoods, which have the potential to add so much to the competence and passion that children, youth, and adults might bring to their life activities, aren't bounded by where a person lives physically. We show them to be places where people choose to be and are invited to join. We show them to be moveable and transferable so that people can and do take them with them when they leave home, in effect taking their home community with them.

Of course, this isn't the usual way of thinking about communities and neighborhoods. And because we are still asking you to take an alternate view of very possible experiences, we offer multiple pieces of data to tell these stories, each with different sources and degrees of error. We make no claim to being able to produce an effect size or even a significance test for participation in ATDP. But we do have considerable information that readers can weigh for themselves.

Our information comes in two general forms: reactive and nonreactive measures (Webb, Campbell, Schwartz, Sechrest, & Grove, 1981). Our reactive measures are the various surveys and questionnaires the program has used over the years. Our nonreactive measures are diverse, which adds to the validity of our accounts, but they also are largely unsystematic. They include unsolicited comments—paper and e-mail letters, stories students or parents tell when they visit the members of the staff and their teachers, and stories ATDP teachers tell about what they have learned from former students. They also include external evaluations done by people who have supported groups of students through the program. In short, we offer a medley of information, hoping that the weight and diversity of the information offer a fair and interesting picture of what we know about the after-effects of attending the program. Over and over they underscore how central a role their own version of the ATDP community has played in shaping the choices they've made in creating their lives.

We don't know whose voices we are missing in our accounts of students' experiences with the program, and we don't know what stories those students would tell. We do know that a small number of students withdraw. In 2006 with about 1,400 students completing Secondary Division, 21 withdrew after the program began. With just 1,000 students in Elementary Division, a few students withdrew because of illness or a family emergency. And some withdrew because they just didn't like the program. The following is typical of the last group.

Some years ago a father and son came to the director to tell her that the son was withdrawing from the program. When she asked why, the upset father said, "He's spending way too much time on his homework. I told him that he wouldn't have much homework."

"Oh, let's see how many hours of homework per class is listed in the catalog for Algebra I. It says 7 to 10 hours per class session. How many hours is your son spending?"

"That's it: 7."

"But that's what the catalog lists."

"I know that. But I told him, 'That's for *regular* kids. If it takes *them* 7 hours, you'll be done in 1 hour, tops.'"

That's just it. Our belief is that everyone at ATDP is a regular kid and everyone has to put in sweat equity. Everyone at ATDP is present to learn things that at the time they'd be unlikely to learn elsewhere—this includes the outstanding experts who teach there. So, it's not the ideal place for students and parents looking for a restful vacation or searching for a spotlight for a solo performance on center stage.

THOSE WHO CHOOSE TO RETURN TO THE COMMUNITY, AND THOSE WHO CHOOSE TO REMAIN IN IT

What do students do with their lives and say about the program after a summer with ATDP? The first answer is that many of them return to take another course the following summer. Students and their parents express their opinions with their feet. The value of the experience can be measured to some degree by the fact that in any given summer a large number of the students are returning students. Some students age out of the program, and others move away. But even some of those come back. Often students skip a year of attendance since there are many other wonderful things to do during the summer and ATDP encourages its students to participate in them; but they return again later.

As with the Nobless family (see Chapter 5), it is not unusual for one child after another in a family to spend several summers at ATDP. Kee, the child of an immigrant family of very modest means, and Kyle, the child of an educationally and economically privileged family, both followed siblings into the program. Kee began before entering Grade 7 (already an exception, but he had attended Elementary Division previously) with Introduction to Geometric Thinking, and then, year after year, added Introduction to Programming, Public Speaking, Writing for High School, the Practice of Law, and Intensive Lab Chemistry. Kyle began at the end of Grade 7 (not having attended Elementary Division first) with Foundations of Algebra, and then added Algebra 1, Geometry, Dynamic Chemistry, and AP Biology. In 2005, finally expanding his math and science pattern of choices, Kyle also enrolled in AP English the same summer that he took Robotics.

Interestingly, there are students who have spent more years with the program than Kee or Kyle, yet are not recorded as doing so because of the nature of their participation. Some youth began as students and then became teaching assistants, or mentor-tutors, or part-time office staff, or even, eventually, program instructors. One former student, who now is an ATDP instructor, also teaches at a small high school during the regular school year and has taken to bringing a group of his high school students to the program. He claims that his students, by virtue of being *his* students, are program *legacies*. So, even without logo T-shirts or baseball caps, ATDP seems to have a highly visible school tie. The director and staff have come to know very well some families who have sent child after child to the program. In one extreme case a young man came to the program from the Central Valley as a 12-year-old and spent multiple summers in ATDP, and was then followed by three younger brothers. Now his own child Cristina has just finished her fifth year in the Elementary Division, and was joined in 2007 by a sibling and a cousin. Additionally, as many other ATDP students do, Cristina and her mother, who teaches high school in the Central Valley, have invited friends to come with them to Berkeley, so some of her friends are returning for their second or third years. That's what we call an example of choices freely made.

Students, and their parents, "return" to the program even years after they have completed their last course, keeping the program staff and teachers apprised of their life's adventures and reminiscing about their ATDP ex-

periences. One example is the following e-mail note written by a former
ATDP teacher (who is now a professor in the Midwest) to the program
director about a former student:

> To: Nina
> Fr: Elaine Quintana
> Subject: Thought you'd get a kick out of this
>> Hi Nina!
>> I hope this finds you well. I just got this e-mail from a former
>> ATDP student of mine who went on to Berkeley, and is now getting
>> her MPH at University of Washington:
>> "I actually want to let you [the teacher] know that I'm continu-
>> ally amazed at how useful taking Social Science Research Lab 8 or 9
>> summers ago continues to be! Since everything we read is a journal
>> article, we're always critiquing all the different components of the
>> paper (background, methods, etc.) and I don't think I've ever gotten
>> any kind of formal introduction to each section except in your class!
>> Sure, I probably would have figured it out by now, but I think that
>> summer was just so helpful! How to lie with statistics, how to
>> conduct lit searches. . . . I still use all of those tools! And last quarter
>> I did note taking for some focus groups we conducted . . . and I
>> totally remembered how to look for nonverbal gestures and com-
>> munication, also from being in your class! Anyway, this is getting
>> very long and rambly, but I thought I'd share that with you!"
>> Things are good with me—work . . . is interesting, and a good
>> balance with new parenthood. Dana is now 9 months old!
>> Hugs,
>> Elaine

And here is a note from a parent about her son.

> Hey Lloyd, Nina and everyone at ATDP!
>> Hope you remember us. Ronald attended for about 4 or 5 sum-
>> mers! Well, he is now 25 years old and working for the hedge fund
>> group. . . . He is going to go to grad school this summer . . . while
>> working! Go figure! Must have been that great education that he got
>> with you all. [His] ultimate goal is to get a PhD in Math and teach at
>> the university level. Personally, I am thrilled that he is continuing his
>> education. Given where we started out, this was always my dream.
>> But there was never a guarantee that he'd get there.
>> Hope you are all doing great. I think of you often and fondly. I
>> will never be able to thank you enough for what ATDP did for my

son's education, personal development, and self-esteem. You are the BEST!

   Hugs and Kisses, Jacqueline Foster

And from another parent, again many years after her daughter's participation:

My name is Katharine Chang and you helped my daughter, Nicole, get into ATDP. . . . As a result she fell in love with Cal, attending undergrad and grad courses there, finishing a PhD in May. She's now an Assistant Prof . . . in Asian languages. I just want to say thanks for that initial help and the great program you have there.

WOULD YOU LIKE TO RETURN? WOULD YOU RECOMMEND THE CLASS TO A FRIEND?

We are uncertain about what keeps students coming back. We have survey data, and we have anecdotal reports, but their impetus seems too complicated to be explained simply. Yet we can share what information we have. We begin with students' responses to a question asked each year on the End-of-Program Survey: "If you were able to, would you attend this Program next summer?"

   In 2002, 80.6% of the respondents said *Yes*. We know that a great many students do not return, but we believe that the positive responses to the prompt signify something important about the nature of the experience the youth have just had. Something about the experience is sufficiently positive to be seen as worth doing again. The students' voices seem to indicate that returning to ATDP is a choice, not something the youth are pressured into by parents.

   There is a similar question on the form that asks if the student would recommend the class they have just completed to a friend. This question generates even more positive responses: on the order of 80–90% of the respondents any given year, for any given ATDP department, choose *Yes*. (Some *No* responses are interesting, but we don't know if they're actually informative: "My friends aren't as smart as I am.") Even students who may voice some hesitation about taking a second (or third or fourth) class the following summer, are quite confident that the class they just took was valuable for them and would be valuable for a friend. They are certain that their teacher and their classmates made the experience valuable. Clearly, ATDP classes are not something forced on youth or something that they do without enthusiasm.

Big Fish from Little Ponds Willingly Enter a Huge Pond

One of the more interesting pairs of responses on the End-of-Program-Survey suggests that the draw of the program has little to do with ATDP helping the students to feel smart. The survey poses the following two prompts: (1) Rate yourself in academic ability compared with others in this (ATDP) course.

(2) At your regular school last year how do you think you ranked with all other students your age? The choices are the same for both prompts: *among the best, above average, average, below average, among the poorest.* However, the mean response for ranking in comparison with other ATDP students always is significantly lower than ranking in comparison students at their home schools. In other words, the students routinely indicate that the academic challenge from their classmates feels much greater at ATDP than in the school they attend during the academic year. This result is predictable, of course, since ATDP, according to the students, has a much higher concentration of especially able students than does their own school, public or private. Predictable also because there is a well-studied phenomenon called the "big-fish-little-pond" effect on academic self-concept (Marsh, Hau, & Carven, 2004; Zeidner & Schleyer, 1999) in which gifted children find themselves intimidated when they leave their small pond, or local school, to attend a specialized school with other gifted students.

And indeed, students at ATDP report feeling more like a "little fish in a big pond." Across all groups, across all courses, they report having to swim like mad to keep up with the school. The expectation would be that students—especially students from low-performing schools—would respond negatively to the prospect of returning to a situation that causes "heightened evaluative" anxiety and threatens to yield lower grades (Zeidner & Schleyer, 1999, pp. 319, 321). Further, "attending selective educational frameworks should lead to reduced academic self-concept for students of all ability levels" (p. 321). We would say *performance levels,* but the point remains the same.

But very few respond the way the father and son did in the story we told earlier. The End-of-Program Survey results lead us to believe that a large majority of ATDP students, as a whole, leave each summer with fond memories of their teachers and their classes. The less structured data we have help fill out the picture. Why do they keep coming back?

How do the students describe their experiences with ATDP in their own words? Here is Mike (the student who has 11 years with the program), speaking to the 2005 orientation audience:

> I never had a teacher who was not enthusiastic, supportive, and caring. . . . In each class I had fun, expanded my horizons, and I

learned to look at the world in a different way. . . . Mr. Engle has changed my life. . . . I come from a well-read family, we spend a lot of time talking about ideas. The things we read in class, the conversations there have made us think about *everything* differently.

And here is Phoebe, sending e-mail to her teacher during the middle of a summer experience:

I want you to know how much I have enjoyed all of your classes and the time we have spent talking. You are the most inspiring teacher I have ever had. I promise I will continue working on my German after ATDP to make up for the fact that I concentrated so much on my acting and Latin. Autem, you have given me this summer something that I know will become a lasting passion. I love Latin more than just about anything I have come across recently.

Yvonne wrote to her teacher a week or so after the end of AP Biology.

This class has taught me more than biology. It taught me sincere devotion to doing the best I can throughout the course. I seriously have not worked so hard at any other class than this biology course. Throughout the two months, everyday consisted of biology and nothing else. Coming out of this class with an 89.4 is not exactly the raw score I desired, but I have never been more proud of such a score. I have never been truly proud of my As in high school, but yet, I am ironically proud of my B+ in ATDP biology. In my high school, an A comes easily in most classes if the homework is completed and the tests are passed. However, in this biology course, completion does not give the points. True understanding is necessary to pass the class. . . . Everything in this biology class taught me to always do the best I can. . . . Thank you.

One of the most eloquent descriptions of the ATDP experience that we have ever read came from a former student, when he was a freshman at college, who wrote to the program director and the director's ATDP teacher-husband about his transition to college.

When I think about why I feel so settled at college, I'm reminded of what drew me back to ATDP over the summers. Being surrounded by people who are at once intelligent and humble, curious and generous, and working in an environment where learning is valued for its own sake and not as a means to a practical end—there are very few places where these things are true, and ATDP and my college are among them. I owe both of you a profound debt of gratitude for being there over the summers, for giving me something to look forward to during the school year. I feel like a very fortunate person.

Some former students tell us much about their ATDP experiences without ever doing so directly. For example, they write the program director to ask for a former teacher's e-mail address in order to write the teacher for help with a college essay. They stop by the ATDP offices to chat with the director or their favorite member of the staff even years after their summer(s) with the program. They send holiday cards, they send e-mail reporting on experiences in college, and they call to discuss job opportunities or graduate school possibilities. They send photos of their babies and announce the year they'll be ready to attend Elementary Division. We believe that these actions say much about the quality of the experiences the former students had with ATDP.

Former Teachers Praise the Program, Too

Teachers write also, even years after their work with the program. Recall the earlier report with a former teacher writing to the program director to share an e-mail from a former student. And here, 13 years after he moved out of the area, another teacher wrote:

> My ATDP years remain the highlight of my teaching career. I absolutely enjoyed those summers, the kids, the collegial staff, the wonderful, professional conversations with my fellow teachers, the great field trips—all of it. You get the credit, thank you. . . . ATDP will forever remain the paragon of great teaching: something to aim for.

Still another former teacher, who moved away more recently, sent an e-mail about an internship in Washington, D.C. She closed her note this way:

> I hope you're doing well and that the ATDP staff is all geared up for another great Brigadoon-like summer. Also, I hope you won't mind if I send a few e-mails or call you about questions I have about gifted ed policy in the future. I like learning from experts =).

IF RESPONSES ARE SO SIMILAR, CAN STUDENTS' BACKGROUNDS REALLY BE THAT DIFFERENT?

The students at ATDP in any given summer may represent as many as 300 middle schools and high schools. These schools vary enormously in all the ways one might imagine. The school with the largest number of ATDP students most summers—School A—is frequently listed among the eminent public high schools in the nation. The school described itself this way on its Web page in 2005:

> Underlying [our] philosophy of education is the resolve that the young people of [this city] continue to enjoy their traditional option of attending a college preparatory public high school. The emphasis requires an instructional program that promotes sound intellectual and aesthetic values while providing opportunities for self-discipline and individual decision making.

During the summer of 2004, 59 students from this esteemed high school enrolled in ATDP. The school's total enrollment is close to 3,000.

Many years ago, when students from this school began attending ATDP, the students most likely came without the knowledge of their school administrators, as their principal disapproved of out-of-school education. Only in recent years, in acknowledgment of the large number of students from this school at ATDP each summer, the ATDP staff have initiated informal relations with the school administration and some of its teachers. Just as parents work very hard to secure a place for their children in this selective public high school, they also value participation in ATDP and in other academic programs across the United States. It is not unusual for a student from this school to perform in a musical competition at Carnegie Hall or to travel all over the world during summer vacation. Others find summer internships in laboratories.

The second largest number of ATDP students in 2004 and many other summers, come from an outreach program that serves California's Central Valley area of Coalinga-Huron-Avenal (CHA). In the summer of 2004, there were 54 students at ATDP from this small set of two Central Valley school districts with combined high school enrollments of about 1,400. Over the years, for many high school students from these valley communities, the choice for summer activities has been between working in the fields alongside their parents or foregoing the needed money and attending ATDP, or "going to Berkeley" as the students call it.

That same year a participating middle school from this area, sending the largest number of CHA students to ATDP, describes itself this way on its Web page:

Our mission is to provide all [our] students the opportunity to be
ready and prepared to enter high school without remediation
instruction, based on scores of at or above the CAT-6 [*sic*], as well as
in new performance and state content standards.

Thus, so far as academic orientations of their respective schools and
life circumstances, ATDP students do come from a wide, wide range of
different backgrounds.

The ATDP director and staff have worked closely with educators from
this valley community for 20 years, building a collaboration that serves well
both the youth in the community and the larger group of youth at ATDP. The
first summer after the conversation began, just one student from the community enrolled in ATDP (it is he who now has two children attending Elementary Division). Since then, 263 students have taken part in the program. We
will have more to share about this collaboration later in this chapter.

A COMMUNITY OF GIFTS, GLADLY SHARED

And so it is as you might expect: With the 300 or so schools represented
by ATDP students, some schools are very strong academically and other
schools are weak academically in one or more respects. Some are large,
some are small, some are public (actually, 75–80% are public) and some
are private or parochial, some feature special programs and others are more
general comprehensive schools, and recently some few students are home-
schooled in high school. Students from the range of schools one would find
in a very large geographic area come to ATDP classes together for 6 weeks
each year. They meet people with similar intellectual interests but quite
different life experiences. The youth learn to walk comfortably in worlds
larger than their home communities.

This academic adventure brings people from widely differing life circumstances together, expands their world of possibilities, and is of benefit
to all. As we write this we know some readers are asking, "You keep saying that. Can't you be more specific? What exactly do you mean? Can you
give an example?"

Yes, we can, by sharing LaKeesha's story (Gabelko & Sosniak, 2002).
LaKeesha first came to ATDP at the end of eighth grade through an outreach program with a nearby large urban school district. That summer she
was one of three ATDP students from her middle school, a school that
served predominantly minority students and was beset by all kinds of
educational, social, and financial problems. While her two friends enrolled
in Introduction to the Writing Process, LaKeesha enrolled in Shakespeare

as Theatre. This was LaKeesha's first year in ATDP, it was her first contact with students from other school districts, from different racial and ethnic groups, and with different life experiences.

Initially, LaKeesha felt very uncomfortable, both with the presence of so many strange faces in her ATDP class and with the unfamiliar sound of Elizabethan English in class. She wanted to turn and run. But she didn't. She found herself connecting quickly with the instructor, a well-known local actor and director with a contagiously passionate love of her craft and of her subject, and a wonderful Irish accent of her own. But even a connection with the instructor could not make LaKeesha feel comfortable or confident with her classmates. In fact, the prospect of a class trip for an evening performance of Shakespeare held in a park in an affluent suburb caused LaKeesha to try to withdraw from the course.

LaKeesha told the instructor that her mother would not give permission for her to attend the performance because in her neighborhood no one her age was allowed to be out after dark. Another student, Elizabeth— White and, according to LaKeesha, "at least a planet removed" from LaKeesha's own life—overheard the conversation and chimed in that her mother tended to be exactly like that, too. But Elizabeth had been able to convince her mother that it would be fine, since the performance was outside and there was enough space for the whole family to come and have a picnic supper on the grass. Elizabeth said she would have her mother call LaKeesha's mother and not only convince her that it was safe but tell her that they would call for LaKeesha and bring her home.

LaKeesha said that this put her into a real panic. "No way was I going to have this rich White girl come to my house. No way was I going to some rich White park. . . . All I knew was that I had to get out of this mess." At first LaKeesha said that Elizabeth's mother couldn't phone because she didn't have a telephone. But, according to LaKeesha, this just made Elizabeth more persistent.

In the end, LaKeesha did go to the Shakespeare-in-the-Park performance, and she says she was close to panic the whole evening. Even the presence of a guidance counselor from her own school, who was also an ATDP counselor, did not ease her discomfort. Because LaKeesha and Elizabeth were attending the performance together, the instructor assigned them to learn and perform together a scene from the play they had attended; Elizabeth was to play Celia, and LaKeesha was to play Rosalind. To LaKeesha, this meant that even if she survived the evening, the worst was yet to come.

LaKeesha, who was the top student in her grade at her home school, says that she was shocked to learn that Elizabeth not only was having difficulty remembering her lines but also was having problems with the language of Shakespeare.

I couldn't believe it. Lizzy didn't even get the jokes in our scene. I had to explain them to her over and over. I was just shocked. In class, I had to take her outside and say all of her lines for her and have her copy me so she didn't act a fool in front of everybody. Even at the performance, where I was signed up to be in four different scenes, I had to just about feed her the lines in our scene and in the other scene she was in. In that one, I learned her lines just by hearing her rehearse a couple of times. . . . This just wasn't the way I expected things to be.

LaKeesha returned to ATDP for three more summers. Then she went to college. ATDP (and Shakespeare) had taught her lessons that she had not anticipated.

By the time I got to college, to tell the truth, I didn't even remember that I had ever been intimidated by people just because of their color and hometown. When I got to [college], I was taken aback when my classmates, including my first roommate, tried to stereo-type me. . . . I kept thinking to myself: "Well, this sure ain't ATDP." But they eventually got it and things are going very well.

At ATDP, academic engagement often seems to trump race, class and gender in how students think about themselves and how they think about others. Again and again, alumni report that they learned an enormous amount from their fellow students. They particularly appreciated the diversity of student life experiences that helped them understand themselves better and feel more comfortable in the new communities they encountered when they moved beyond high school and left their family home. When asked to list the most important contribution ATDP made to their lives, alumni who had attended 3 or more years said that it was the opportunity to learn and become friends with students from different backgrounds and life circumstances.

MEMBERSHIP HAS BENEFITS NOT AVAILABLE TO VISITORS

For many years, the City A school district sponsored African American and Latino students' participation in ATDP. The collaboration began with 11 African American students and, over time, included many more racial and linguistic minority group students—as many as 160 students one summer. The district's goal was to increase equity and school performance for their targeted students. Initially, the district's leaders thought that students should just "visit" ATDP, that is, attend for one summer only as seventh graders. The district requested that their sponsored students attend class together. In other words, the district's vision did not include seeing their students as part of ATDP, but rather as being exposed to a college campus.

This venture dates so far back that it began in the last days of the Gifted Program. The ATDP program staff wanted so much for the program to become more diverse that they even agreed to "introductory-only" classes, which meant that the classes included only City A students, from various schools in the City A district. The district also requested that teachers from the district be hired to teach district-sponsored students. The district seemed to be frightened to begin a venture that was beyond a school district field trip to the Berkeley campus.

As the district leadership changed within a couple of years, the one-year-only, seventh-grade-only policy went by the wayside. The district, however, still wanted their students to realize that it was their school district that had sent them to the program, and wanted their students to stay together. That may be a field trip of longer duration, but it still offers only a visit to ATDP and not membership in it.

The City A students were no longer required to eat lunch together because it was no longer practical. But the students continued to be together in a separate summer support program created for them, and they traveled together on public transit. By the time LaKeesha came to ATDP (see above for LaKeesha's story), the school district began to see the benefits of broader participation beyond paying visits, and a new ATDP counselor (from LaKeesha's school) encouraged City A students to join ATDP fully. The counselor, Ms. Taylor, had grown up on the campus of a prestigious historically Black college, where her mother had headed the student health services. Consequently, she had wonderful stories to share about colleges and college life and encouraged students to explore the campus and to get to know many new friends.

So, with Ms. Taylor's support, combined with additional academic and social support from the program, between the years 1990 and 1998 inclusive, this group of nontraditional students became ATDP returnees at a rate slightly higher than the rate for students outside of the group and without additional supports (Worrell, Szarko, & Gabelko, 2001, p. 82).

THE STUDENTS VOTED WITH THEIR FEET; WHAT DID THEY AND THEIR DISTRICT SAY?

Members of the City A school district prepared their own evaluation reports for the summer experience, and routinely these were very positive.

ATDP provides an intense, stimulating academic experience for our students sponsored by the school district's Integration Office. They engage in passionate scholarly dialogue from abstract mathematical reasoning to bioluminescence with hands-on experiences that support the learning. This experience encourages them to pursue more challenging classes at their regular schools and investigate postsecondary educational opportunities with confidence. (1998–99 evaluation report)

Indeed, the students did seem to learn about more challenging educational experiences. One student said,

"Classes just aren't this tough during the school year. We need to be able to get our heads into this kind of study where our teachers respect our ideas and comments." (in 1998–99 report)

Another student reported that ATDP "helped me glimpse a future that had been hidden from me, namely, 'college, university, serious intellectual work'" (1998–99 report). Another student described ATDP as "a life-altering experience" (2001–02 report). And still another was quoted as saying:

"There was a huge workload, but it was totally worth it. The things I learned are showing through right now. Because right now in math we're being introduced to things I learned last summer. Many of the students are having trouble, whereas I'm doing really well." (in 2001–02 report)

The district evaluators also visited classes. One that particularly caught the eye of an evaluator was a Marine Biology lab. This class included three Latino and two African American district-sponsored students in the class of 23—a vast improvement over the earlier field trip/visitor days for City A students. On the day of his observation, he found the class working in small groups dissecting fish:

The biologist/teacher was very busy helping students identify key parts of the anatomy and probing the students about their knowledge of its function. Students were readily making comparisons to their own research papers. One of the ICUSD students wrote his [research paper] on bioluminescence and the lantern fish.

The City A effort continued and even flourished through several more administrations, but after close to 16 years in operation, a change in district priorities with financial woes led the district to withdraw from the collaboration. The combination of the two took their toll on the effort and the collaboration ended. Without sponsorship, the support ended for textbook and travel expenses that the students had received from their school district. That was a loss. It was also a loss to ATDP when the district stopped sharing information about ATDP with its schools, site administrators, and students.

However, ATDP teachers and staff had left impressions on the students, their parents, and some of their teachers. ATDP mailed information and applications directly to students who had attended during the 2 previous years, inviting them to return. So, while in greatly decreased numbers, former district-sponsored students continued to attend, applying the same way as students from different school districts do and choosing their courses consistent with their own interests and not school district priorities of enhancing reading and math proficiency.

One of the ATDP staff began working with counselors and teachers in individual City A public schools. Today, ATDP, without the district's knowledge has its own outreach program with seven of its public middle schools. In the summer of 2005, 71 students from these schools took part in the program. Of course many other students from other City A schools also attend ATDP each summer, without any special relationships between ATDP their schools. But the most impressive part of the legacy of ATDP's relationship with students who had been sponsored by the district's Integration Office is that an ATDP alumna and her mother, a bilingual classroom aide in a City A school, began their own outreach program at the mother's elementary school and have been sending second-language-learning Latino students to ATDP ever since. Their first ATDP-er, who began in kindergarten when they started the program, graduated from high school in 2007, never missing a summer at ATDP and bringing his younger siblings along after him.

GIFT OF COMMUNITY, COMMUNITY OF GIFTS: BELONGING, CREATING, CONFERRING ON OTHERS

In Chapter 5 and earlier in this chapter, we have made reference to an outreach project with students from Coalinga-Huron-Avenal (CHA). This is the longest and strongest of the ATDP partnership efforts. We can be most specific about what students say about ATDP and do after the program for this CHA outreach group consisting of students from Central Valley farming towns who have come to Berkeley and ATDP each summer for more than 20 years now. In the summer of 2005, 44 students from

CHA attended the program. The CHA House directors—all adults from the community—decided that 44 was too large a group of teens to live with for 6 weeks (no one even talks about the summer that Mrs. Mellor and the house parents lived with 54 teens!) and vowed to cut the size by at least 10. But there are too many dedicated, hardworking, delightful youth in the CHA schools who compel the CHA House directors to say, "Please join us in our adventure."

ATDP has been working with and following this group from the start. The youth complete the same application forms as any others applying to ATDP, but they tend to be entitled to and to receive financial aid in a much greater percentage than youth from any other area. Also, these youth are very strongly encouraged to take part in the support elements of ATDP, such as the learning labs and the one-on-one tutoring. The staff make strong efforts every year to get to know these students personally and to provide leadership and friendship for them during the whole year, not just the summer. That task is made easy by the many unofficial ATDP staff and regular ATDP instructors, themselves CHA alumni, who are at the core of the circle.

For CHA students, invitations into the neighborhood have been extended before the summer began and continue after the summer is over. Their summers at ATDP expand CHA students' map of their neighborhood to include Berkeley and San Francisco, by attending museums and theater performances, walking across the Golden Gate Bridge at 2:00 a.m., having afternoon tea at the most exclusive hotel dining rooms, serving meals at local soup kitchens to homeless people, and volunteering to assist in rebinding revered texts at a local Buddhist monastery. When the students return to the Central Valley, they interact with institutions like the Valley Arts Council and its museums, as well as live local theater productions available in the 200 miles that now join them to San Francisco and beyond.

As of the summer of 2005, we counted 263 CHA students who have taken part in the program since 1989. One hundred and fifty-two of them are old enough to be enrolled in, or even graduated from, college. Shortly we will tell you about their college-going rate and their lives after college. But first it seems important to set the stage, to share something about what might have been expected from these youth based on data from their home school districts.

CHA Demographics and Graduation Rates

When we conducted a Web search in April 2007 for the Coalinga-Huron Joint Unified School District in Fresno County and the Reef-Sunset Unified School District in Kings County, we were able to find information about the school districts and their students beginning from 1992 and continuing to 2006, though Reef-Sunset (Avenal) did not join ATDP until 1999 (see http://www.ed-data.k12.ca.us).

We learned, for example, that the Coalinga-Huron Joint Unified School District had a K–12 enrollment of approximately 3,700 in 1992, and over 15 years had grown to a school enrollment of approximately 4,413 in 2006. In the same year, Reef-Sunset had 2,157 students enrolled in 1992, and 2,584 in 2006. Both districts' school populations were largely Hispanic approximately 65% for Coalinga-Huron and 82% for Reef-Sunset when ATDP began serving students from that community, and the populations have become increasingly more Hispanic over the years to 77% and 86% respectively in 2005–2006. In 2006, over 70% of the districts' students were English learners. Respectively, 65% and 61% of students in each district qualified for free or reduced-price lunch.

Just a small percentage of students graduate from Coalinga-Huron or Reef-Sunset high schools having completed all the courses with a grade of C or better, required for eligibility for the state's public 4-year university systems, University of California (UC) and California State University (CSU). These students are typically called "UC/CSU eligible" high school graduates. Of the 155 Coalinga-Huron students in the high school graduating class of 1992, only 32 students—20.3%—were counted as UC/CSU eligible; in the graduating class of 1996, just 14.8% of the district graduates were UC/CSU eligible. And for the class of 2004, the most recent data available, 21.6 percent of the district graduates were UC/CSU eligible (the highest percentage of any year and 10% higher than the previous year).

Teasing Out the Program Effects

Readers might be interested in comparing these numbers with other schools and school districts. At highly esteemed School A (mentioned earlier in this chapter) with the largest number of ATDP students over the past few years, 87.8% of the graduating class of 2004 were UC/CSU eligible. In the City A district, 56.6% of graduating high school students were UC/CSU eligible, and in the Los Angeles Unified School District 38% of graduates were UC/CSU eligible. In other words, Coalinga-Huron-Avenal students, who are largely Hispanic and largely from poor families, are even less likely to take or pass with a grade of C the courses they need for admission to the state universities in California than students from the urban school districts of City A or Los Angeles.

But the Coalinga-Huron-Avenal students who have spent time at ATDP do take these courses and earn good grades, and do go on to graduate from college. Some attend some small colleges nearest to home; others go to the University of California schools and to California State University schools. They also travel from California across the country to attend private colleges and universities with outstanding reputations: Stanford, USC, Yale, Harvard, Mt. Holyoke, Oberlin, Swarthmore, Brown, Cornell, Haverford, Johns Hopkins, MIT, and Wellesley.

We feel confident claiming that ATDP helps turn Coalinga-Huron-Avenal students into college students. The program introduces them to college expectations, and makes it possible and desirable for them to take and complete successfully the UC/CSU high school course requirements. Of the 152 CHA outreach youth who have taken part in ATDP and are now old enough to have applied to college, 6% (9) did not enroll in any post secondary school, 15% (23) attended a two-year institution, and 69% (120) attended a 4-year college or university.

And what of the higher education graduation rate? Many of the youth still are in school. Among the others, 3 have left college without a degree; 7 have earned an AA degree (from a 2-year program); 65 have earned a BA degree (from a 4-year program); 2 have earned an MA degree; 2 have earned MD degrees; 1 has earned a PhD, one is currently enrolled in a PhD program, two are currently enrolled in medical school and others are enrolled in teacher education programs, law school, and other professional programs.

Of course it is important to question whether the Coalinga-Huron-Avenal students who attended ATDP would have gone to college with or without the support of the program. Were they the exceptions who would have proven the rule by their admission to Yale or Swarthmore or Oberlin? We believe this is unlikely, and the students claim that ATDP is the reason behind their success. Well, ATDP and the neighborhood and community of practice begun by Nancy Mellor and actively supported by many of the students' parents, and by the very tight friendships the students formed. These friendships, and the cohorts and subcohorts they subsume, are worthy of serious study, as they began when the students' hometowns were segregated from each other and when the high school where they met reflected that segregation precisely. These friendships initially existed during the summer only, when students from the segregated schools lived together under their CH House flag (no Avenal participation then). And each year on the last day of ATDP they lowered their flag with the benediction "we now go our own ways, to return together next summer." Many such bonds—across and within ethnic groupings—still hold twenty years later.

These youth were path blazers and strong students from the beginning, but they were not initially academically outstanding in the way that students from nationally recognized School A show themselves to be. For example, in 1996, of that school's students at ATDP, 61% scored at or above the 97th percentile in mathematics, in contrast to 11% of CHA students on the same annual state test of academic achievement. Clearly, the CHA youth entered ATDP with lower standardized test scores than did students in the program as a whole. What about more recently? In 2005, the average score for City A High School students at ATDP was at the 95th percentile in mathematics, with 54% scoring at or above the 97th percentile. For the same year, on the same test, the average score for CHA students at ATDP was at the 53rd percentile in mathematics, with 5% at or above the 97th percentile and 29% at or above the 90th percentile. In other words, the ATDP students from Coalinga-Huron look much like their counterparts in their small Central Valley schools except that the ATDP youth have gone on to college in numbers unprecedented for the area and for their own families.

And after college? We do not yet have a complete accounting. But, to date, we have been able to identify as CHA alumni one assistant professor at a research university, two physicians, fifteen teachers, three other educators, six engineers, one city planner, one financial analyst, one banker, one program officer for a foundation in the Valley, one dance troupe leader, one lawyer, three business owners, one nurse, and four members of the military.

If the measure of talent development is some form of celebrity—winning national awards, and being known far beyond one's family and community, or even attending famous colleges and universities—then ATDP gladly comes up short. The CHA students' names would not be on the tip of your tongue. But if the measure of talent development includes going to college when it would not have been predicted, and making responsible and valuable contributions as adults, then ATDP clearly demonstrates its success. ATDP counts as part of that success, even the fact that some parents are following in their children's paths. One dad, inspired by his sons, went to college and then graduate school and now is a dropout-prevention counselor at the middle school his sons attended; the mother of another student has earned a GED twice—first in Spanish and then in English—and now is attending night classes at a community college (with friends whose children also went to ATDP) to study early childhood education and will soon open a licensed bilingual preschool and child care center. The group of parents who had previously worked together in the fields now continue to work together in their new ventures.

When CHA alumni speak publicly about their experiences—as they did, for example, at a reunion evening in July 2003—they almost always remark that before ATDP they thought they would follow family and friends into work in the fields. They thrill in their ability to find a wide range of ways of earning a livelihood that bring them happiness and greater financial resources for their families. They speak of the work involved with pride rather than annoyance. "Francisco was our math expert; Geraldo was our writing expert; Cristina was an engineer from the day we got to ATDP—she was always organizing everyone and telling them what they needed to do. When kids are supposed to talk about soccer and baseball, we would actually be talking about class." Reminiscing about long nights doing homework, one young man reported that "my body was exhausted but my mind was like . . . this is awesome." One of the early members of the CHA group spoke about the experience as an "opportunity that came with responsibilities. I had new ways of looking at my life and influencing my decisions . . . and my brothers followed me here, and then to college."

More privately, some in the group wonder about the classmates they left behind. How did the two roads diverge so that some went to college and others had not considered it as worthwhile? We trouble over this question too. At the same time, we celebrate their personal accomplishments and the benefits they've brought to their hometowns. They have infused their own K–12 schools with more than dreams of diffuse possibilities, they've set the next cohorts on a path with certificated, bona fide guides.

On a recent visit to a fourth-grade classroom in an elementary school in Avenal, when the director introduced herself to the students, Oscar raised his hand, exclaiming, "Wait! Are you Nina-from-Berkeley? You know my mother and my sister. I'm Oscar. I'm supposed to go to Berkeley in the seventh grade. I think I need to go now. I'll ask my mom if I can go because it's time for me to see the world." As adults are wont to do, both his mother and the district superintendent said "No! Not until seventh grade." We think that it was worth the try.

EVEN WITH THE BEST INTENTIONS, SCHOOLS CAN'T DO IT ALL

While trips to Berkeley can wait until the end of seventh grade, rich educational opportunities cannot. Even students as able, dedicated, and accomplished as fourth grader Oscar suffer the consequences of the lack of deep academic choices found in rich neighborhoods. As he already knows, there's a big world out there with terrific things to offer.

Indeed, for the more advantaged children and youth, especially, education outside of school walls and outside of school time frequently is consistent with school goals, perhaps in ways that make the schools appear to add more value to students' lives than they really do. Young children in many homes learn to count, recite the alphabet, and write their names before they enter school. They learn colors and shapes, nursery rhymes, and the idea that most books in the United States are read from left to right and that we read the black part and not the white part on a page. They come to school with vocabularies that support work across the school subjects. Over the years they learn—outside of school—about geography, history, science, and economics. They come prepared for school learning (bringing paper and pencils, rulers, and appropriate ideas about school work) and school testing (sometimes with many hours of practice supplied by or paid for by their parents). In many homes children and youth are introduced to books, newspapers, and magazines, and the bodies of knowledge that come with these resources. In these and many other ways learning in and outside of school often are so linked we can't tell where one ends and the other begins (Sosniak, 1995).

PLEASE CONSIDER THE 91% SOLUTION: RICH LEARNING, INSIDE AND OUTSIDE OF CLASSROOMS

The development of talent—academic or otherwise—cannot depend solely on work done in schools. Education is so much larger than schooling. Even if schools were enormously successful in the tasks they set for themselves and the tasks others set for them, the "risk and opportunity in the non-school hours" (Carnegie Corporation, 1992) are far too substantial to leave unaccounted for and unaccountable. Furthermore, given that students between kindergarten and Grade 12 spend only 9% of their lives in school, which is a low dose of schooling in relation to the 91% of their lives children and youth spend outside of school, we can hardly justify holding schools alone responsible for what students know and can do, or for what they don't know and can't do.

We know full well that the academic achievement gap increases during the summer. It couldn't be otherwise. School is in session 180 days of the year, but education takes place on all 365 days. Children lucky enough to go to schools in the most educationally advantaged communities typically are also most educationally advantaged during the summer and during all the breaks from school. We must create opportunities to use big chunks of that 91% of their time to benefit all students, but most especially those presently denied the possibility of rich educational experiences outside of school.

That 91% solution, especially during the summer, permits self-supporting programs such as ATDP to bring all students together in one place, at one time, and for one reason: to learn within an intellectual community. ATDP pays its own bills from tuition income, including covering financial aid through internal subsidies. It permits many things to happen that are presently unlikely to be possible elsewhere.

As in the analogy to Social Security that Daniel Perlstein gave in Chapter 4, all students need ATDP experiences, and having middle-class and upper-class families who are able to pay tuition—in amounts that correspond favorably to child care fees in our area—permits children from low-income homes to participate just as actively. Children from the educational underclass definitely benefit more from the ATDP experience. But, when ATDP alumni are asked to state the most important contribution ATDP made to their preparation for college, the most frequently mentioned benefit is "learning and making friends with people I could not have met at my school or in my neighborhood."

The program works best when it is, albeit informally, congruent with classroom approaches and values. ATDP consistently acknowledges the outstanding contributions made by spectacular individual teachers during the school year. We've made reference to student triumphs and extraordinary experiences made available in Rafe Esquith's (2003, 2007) classroom, and one of us is old enough to have seen firsthand the magic created by William Johntz's teaching of mathematics to students from low-income families and communities which is described perfectly by Asa Hilliard III (in Perry et al., 2003, p. 133). Rhona Weinstein (2002) has permitted us to experience the joy of being a student in Mrs. Kay's classroom, one of the examples she gives of schooling at its best. Weinstein hits the mark when she shows that the best schooling experiences are ones that expand and extend students' lives: "The boundaries of this classroom and the opportunities for relationship were . . . able to expand to include parents, other classes, and the outside world" (p. 137).

Anything Is Possible in the Good Old Summertime

Why do so many decision makers act as if students with few resources can accomplish as much in 9% of their time—the in-school time—as students from privileged families accomplish using that 9% plus big chunks of the additional 91% available? Why should some be expected to be able to learn it all in that 9% in-school time when the others have an additional 91% time to develop their learning? Further, when decision makers, at all levels, do talk about out-of-regular-school time for students without sufficient resources, their conversation focuses far more often than not on remediation. And in those few times that it's not about remediation, it's about interventions (activities intended to forestall the need for future remediation). That leaves a world of possibilities to be considered for summer vacations and other outside-of-school times.

Yet in the majority of circumstances in which outside-of-school life may be supportive or may be antithetical to it, students are still not helped to make connections. They are not helped to understand how academic considerations relate to one another or what their purposes are. At the same time, though, summer is a perfect time for putting things together and figuring things out. These months—adding up to years over students' childhood and adolescence lives—could stand to make personal and purposeful the 9% of their time spent in regular school.

A Full School Year of Learning Isn't a Full Year of Learning

Presently available only to some, such out-of-school activities make it possible for children and youth to learn things they cannot learn in school, things that can have important influences on their school learning. Not surprisingly, the distribution of such opportunities is such that during this out-of-school time, the gap in conventional achievement increases. Karl Alexander and Doris Entwisle found that children in poverty who began first grade in 1982, contrary to expectations, did make a year of progress for each year in school, but that "the long summer break is especially hard for disadvantaged children" (Schemo, 2006, p. 1). The children they studied returned to school the following fall to see the value of their year's growth greatly diminished by the experiences and activities of the others (see also Lareau, 2004).

Michael Apple (1996), among others, shows clearly that it is "dangerously naive" (p. 70) to expect that schools can be the sole providers of solutions so deeply rooted in societal problems of poverty and lack of democracy, in their many manifestations (some of which we discussed in Chapter 4). Apple warns that "unless we take a new, whole society based, view of these problems, all of which do manifest in the classroom and all of which do broaden achievement gaps, . . . we shall simply be unable to respond adequately to the need of youth in the United States, beyond providing an endless series of short-lived placebos" (p. 70).

We agree wholeheartedly with Apple's statement. But expanding our view to include outside-of-school experiences in which unserved or underserved children and youth are supported in developing their academic frames of mind, we see that there are many untapped opportunities and choices that can easily be provided. We can also see that so long as our children do not have the opportunity to work and learn together, we as a school district, community, or nation, stand little chance of even approaching the democratic goals we espouse.

This same education that increases the achievement gap during the summer is education richly construed that builds wonderful experiences that matter more than what can be measured 8 weeks later. Yet at the same time, it still makes all the more measurable that which schools and policy makers deem important.

Through their "91% activities," children and youth can acquire content knowledge that is better directed and more purposeful than their 9% ones. It makes new vocabulary necessary, and the ideas that merely float around in school textbooks and on school tests are now purposeful. They learn about personal *goals*. They can learn to work with others to accomplish goals; they can learn how to practice purposefully; and they learn the value of initiative. In so doing, they can experience firsthand the benefits that accrue through persistence. They begin to imagine possibilities for their years to come, and they develop aspirations. Summer activities weave in and out of school learning in ways that make it difficult in rich educational environments to tell whether learning in school or out of school is driving success in the other arena.

We must come to understand that outside-of-school environments, be they extraordinary or common, are created by those who inhabit them. These environments can be built with the resources available. Consequently, it is entirely reasonable to expect that interested communities can already create exceptional conditions for young people from all backgrounds regardless of traditionally accepted constraints. Because the people, the place, and the time are all outside of the usual ideas of who learns where and with whom, and because everything is new for all who participate, the assumption becomes "if you're here it's because you want to do new things and meet people you can't meet at home—people just like you."

Well, just as we promised at the very beginning of this book, we haven't provided either a blueprint or a definitive answer. Our hope is that we have offered views and reasons to alter the present discourse on the development of academic talent, of who is and isn't talented, of how academic talent shows itself, and how the development of academic talent must begin even before it appears in commonly recognized forms. We hope that we have shown that everything that happens relative to the development of academic talent happens within a context and that the context that we see as serving children and youth best is one which is offered to full members of communities of practice, be they novices or on their way to becoming experts. We hope that we've convinced you that neighborhoods formed of such communities of practice serve everyone, because such neighborhoods are not bound by geography or circumstance.

We hope that we've shown how 91% solutions make purposeful all of the learning and hard work required of any student and scholar wishing to grow and develop academically and socially. We fervently hope that we've shown that the development of academic talent is supposed to be a joyous enterprise, one with lots of giggles and laughter, and one that meets its promise only when all of us are present and together.

References

Allport, G. W. (1979). *The nature of prejudice* (25th anniversary ed.). New York: Basic Books. (Original work published 1954)

Almond, G., & Verba, S. (1989). *The civic culture: Political attitudes and democracy in five nations.* Newbury Park, CA: Sage. (Original work published 1963)

Apple, M. W. (1996). *Cultural politics and education.* New York: Teachers College Press.

Biesta, G. (2007). Education and the democratic person: Towards a political conception of democratic education [Electronic version]. *Teachers College Record, 109*(3), 740–769.

Blascovich, J., Spencer, S. J., Quinn, D., & Steele, C. M. (2001). African Americans and high blood pressure: The role of stereotype threat. *Psychological Science, 12,* 225–229.

Bloom, B. S. (1982). The role of gifts and markers in the development of talent. *Exceptional Children, 48*(6), 510–521.

Bloom, B. S. (Ed.). (1985). *Developing talent in young people.* New York: Ballantine.

Boulding, K. E. (1961). *The image.* Ann Arbor, MI: Ann Arbor Paperback.

Bridgeman, B., & Wendler, C. (2005, January). *Characteristics of minority students who excel on the SAT and in the classroom.* Princeton, NJ: Educational Testing Service.

Callahan, C. M. (2005, Spring). Identifying gifted students from underrepresented populations. *Theory Into Practice, 44*(2), 98–104.

Carlson, B. (1985). Exceptional conditions, not exceptional talent, produce high achievers. *The University of Chicago Magazine, 78*(1), 18–19, 49.

Carnegie Council on Adolescent Development, Task Force on Youth Development and Community Programs. (1992). *A matter of time: Risk and opportunity in the nonschool hours.* New York: Author.

Carter, P. (2005). *Keepin' it real: School success beyond Black and White.* New York: Oxford University Press.

Clasen, D. R. (1994). Project STREAM: Support, training and resources for educating able minorities. In C. M. Callahan, C. A. Tomlinson, & P. M. Pizzat (Eds.), *Context for promise: Noteworthy practices and innovations in the identification of gifted students* (pp. 1–21). Charlottesville: University of Virginia, Curry School of Education.

Cohen, E. G. (1994). *Designing groupwork: Strategies for the heterogeneous classroom.* New York: Teachers College Press.

Coleman, L. J. (2005). *Nurturing talent in high school.* New York: Teachers College Press.

Cook, D. (2000). We learn to believe in ourselves. *Connect (A Magazine of Teachers' Innovations in K–8 Science and Math)*, *14*(1).

Cox, C. M. (1926). *The early mental traits of three hundred geniuses*. Stanford, CA: Stanford University Press.

Csikszentmihalyi, M., & Robinson, R. E. (1986). Culture, time, and the development of talent. In R. J. Sternberg & J. E. Davidson (Eds.), *Conceptions of giftedness* (pp. 264–284). Cambridge: Cambridge University Press.

Daley, B. (1998). Novice to expert: How do professionals learn? *Adult Education Research Conference (AERC) Proceedings*. Retrieved May 6, 2007, from http://www.adulterc.org/Proceedings/1998/98daley.htm

Dawson, E. M., & Chatman, E. A. (2001). Reference group theory with implications for information studies: A theoretical essay. *Information Research*, *6*(3). Retrieved May 6, 2007, from http://informationr.net/ir/6–3/paper105.html

Dewey, J. (1966). *Democracy and education*. New York: Free Press. (Original work published 1919)

Di Palma, G. (1990). *To craft democracies*. Berkeley: University of California Press.

Dreyfus, H., & Dreyfus, S. (1985). *Mind over machine: The power of human intuition and expertise in the era of the computer*. New York: Free Press.

Dubose, L. (2005, October 7). The din of inequity. *The Texas Observer*. Retrieved May 7, 2007, from http://www.texasobserver.org/article.php?aid=2051

Duckworth, E. (1987). *"The having of wonderful ideas" and other essays on teaching and learning*. New York: Teachers College Press.

Dusek, J. B., & Joseph, G. (1983). The basis of teacher expectancies: A meta-analysis. *Journal of Educational Psychology*, *75*, 177–185.

Engle, S. (2005). *Real kids: Creating meaning in everyday life*. Cambridge, Mass: Harvard University Press.

Ericsson, K. A., Krampe, R. T., & Tesch-Romer, C. (1993). The role of deliberate practice in the acquisition of expert performance. *Psychological Review*, *100*, 363–406.

Esquith, R. (2003). *There are no shortcuts*. New York: Anchor Books.

Esquith, R. (2007). *Teach like your hair's on fire*. New York: Viking.

Feldman, D. H. (with Goldsmith, L. T.) (1986). *Nature's gambit: Child prodigies and the development of human potential*. New York: Basic Books.

Ferguson, R. F. (2002, December). Addressing racial disparities in high-achieving suburban schools [Electronic version]. *NCREL Policy Issues*, *13*, 3–13.

Frasier, M. M., Garcia, J. H., & Passow, A. H. (1995). *A review of assessment issues in gifted education and their implications for identifying gifted minority students* (Research Monograph No. 95204). Storrs: University of Connecticut, National Research Center on the Gifted and Talented.

Gabelko, N. H. (1991). Things they don't teach you in school. *The Educator* (UC at Berkeley Graduate School of Education), *5*(1), 10–13.

Gabelko, N. H., & Michaelis, J. U. (1981). *Reducing adolescent prejudice*. New York: Teachers College Press.

Gabelko, N. H., & Sosniak, L. A. (2002). Someone just like me: When academic engagement trumps race, class, and gender. *Phi Delta Kappan*, *83*(5), 400–405.

Gagné, F. (2003). Transforming gifts into talents: The DMGT as a developmental theory. In N. Colangelo & G. A. Davis (Eds.), *Handbook of gifted education* (3rd ed., pp. 60–74). Boston: Allyn & Bacon.

Gamow, G. (2002). *Mr. Tompkins in Wonderland*. Cambridge, UK: Cambridge University Press. (Original work published 1940)

Garrison, J. (2002, April 21). Irresistible force of a teacher's will. *Los Angeles Times*. Retrieved May 7, 2007, from http://www.angelfire.com/az2/poland/teacher.htm

Getzels, J. W. (1963). Conflict and role behavior in educational settings. In W. W. Charters & N. L. Gage (Eds)., *Readings in the social psychology of education* (pp. 309–318). Boston: Allyn & Bacon.

Getzels, J. W., & Dillon, J. T. (1973). The nature of giftedness and the education of the gifted. In R. M. W. Travers (Ed.), *Second handbook of research on teaching* (pp. 689–731). Chicago: Rand McNally.

Glaser, R., & Chi, M. T. H. (1988). Overview. In M. T. H. Chi, R. Glaser & M. J. Farr (Eds.), *The nature of expertise* (pp. xv–xxviii). Hillsdale, NJ: Erlbaum.

Goffman, E. (1959). *The presentation of self in everyday life*. Garden City, NY: Doubleday, Anchor.

Goffman, E. (1961). *Encounters*. Indianapolis, IN: Bobbs-Merrill.

Golden, D. (2004, April 7). Boosting minorities in gifted programs poses dilemmas—nontraditional criteria lift admissions of Blacks, poor; fear of diluting programs—new focus on the very top. *Wall Street Journal*. Retrieved May 7, 2007, from http://www.greenville.k12.sc.us/gifted/news/2004/wsj.asp

Goldsmith, L. T. (2000). Tracking trajectories of talent: Child prodigies growing up. In R. C. Friedman & B. M. Shore (Eds.), *Talents unfolding: Cognition and development* (pp. 89–122). Washington, DC: American Psychological Association.

Gosa, T. L., & Alexander, K. L. (2007). Family (dis)advantage and the educational prospects of African American youth: How race still matters. *Teachers College Record, 109*(2), 285–321.

Gottfredson, L. S. (2003). The science and politics of intelligence in gifted education. In N. Colangelo & G. A. Davis (Eds.), *Handbook of gifted education* (3rd ed., pp. 24–40). Boston: Allyn & Bacon.

Greene, M. (1989). The question of standards. *Teachers College Record, 91*(1), 9–14.

Grissmer, D., Flanagan, A., & Williamson, S. (1998). Why did the Black-White score gaps narrow in the 1970s and 1980s? In C. Jenks & M. Phillips (Eds.), *The Black-White test score gap* (pp. 182–226). Washington, DC: Brookings Institution Press.

Grotjahn, M. (1954). A review of *The nature of prejudice* by Gordon Allport. *The Psychoanalytic Quarterly, 23*, 604–605.

Gruber, H. E. (1986). The self-construction of the extraordinary. In R. J. Sternberg & J. E. Davidson (Eds.), *Conceptions of giftedness* (pp. 247–263). Cambridge: Cambridge University Press.

Harper, E. P. (2000, Spring). Getting a bang out of Gamow. *GW Magazine, 14*. Retrieved November 6, 2005, from http://www.phys.gwu.edu/index.php?page=getting_a_bang_out_of_gamow/

Havighurst, R. J., Hersey, J., Meister, M., Corning, W. H., & Terman, L. M. (1958). In N. B. Henry (Ed.), *Fifty-seventh yearbook of the National Society for the Study of Education: Part 2. Education for the gifted* (pp. 3–20). Chicago: University of Chicago Press.

Herszenhorn, D. M. (2005, February 17). Schools to add more programs for the gifted. *New York Times*. Retrieved May 7, 2007, from http://select.nytimes.com/ search/restricted/article?res=FA0B13F63D590C778EDDAB0894DD404482

Horowitz, F. D., & O'Brien, M. (1985). Epilogue: Perspectives on research and development. In F. D. Horowitz & M. O'Brien (Eds.), *The gifted and talented: Developmental perspectives.* Washington, DC: American Psychological Association.

Horvat, E. M., & O'Connor, C. (Eds). (2006). *Beyond acting White: Reframing the debate on Black student academic achievement.* New York: Rowman & Littlefield.

Jackson, P. W. (1981). Secondary schooling for the privileged few: A report on a visit to a New England boarding school. *Daedalus, 110*(4), 117–130.

Johnson, K. A. (2000, May 26). *Peer effect on achievement among elementary school students* (Report No. CDA00-6). Washington, DC: Heritage Center for Data Analysis.

Kirk, S. A., Gallagher, J. J., & Anastasiow, N. J. (2000). *Educating exceptional children* (9th ed.). Boston: Houghton Mifflin.

Lareau, A. (2004). *Unequal childhoods: Class, race, and family life.* Berkeley: University of California Press.

Leacock, S. (1921) *Winsome Winnie and other new nonsense novels.* Retrieved May 7, 2007, from http://www.gutenberg.org/etext/20633

Lester, A. E. (2004, May 1). Still separate after all these years? An interview with professor Gary Orfield, co-director of the Civil Rights Project at Harvard. *HGSE News.* Retrieved May 9, 2007, from http://www.gse.harvard.edu/ news/features/orfield05012004.html

Logan, J. (2002). *Separate and unequal: The neighborhood gap for Blacks and Hispanics in metropolitan America.* Albany, NY: The Mumford Center. Retrieved May 9, 2007, from http://mumford.albany.edu/census/SepUneq/SUReport Separate_ and_Unequal.pdf

Marsh, H. W., Hau, K., & Carven, R. (2004, May–June). The big-fish-little-pond effect stands up to scrutiny. *American Psychologist, 59*(4), 269–271.

McCarty, T. L., Lynch, R. H., Wallace, S., & Benally, A. (1991). A classroom inquiry and Navajo learning styles: A call for reassessment. *Anthropology & Education Quarterly, 22,* 42–59.

McClure, C. (2005, March). *Dreyfus model of skill acquisition.* Paper presented at the University of Arizona. Retrieved May 9, 2007, from http://www.ahsc.arizona .edu...odel+of+skill+acquisition%22&hl=en&gl=us&ct=clnk&cd+2&client+ safari

McKown, C., & Weinstein, R. S. (2003). The development and consequences of stereotype consciousness in middle childhood. *Child Development, 74*(2), 498–515.

McNabb, T. (2003). Motivational issues: Potential to performance. In N. Colangelo & G. A. Davis (Eds.), *Handbook of gifted education* (3rd ed., pp. 417–423). Boston: Allyn & Bacon.

Mehan, H., Villanueva, I., Hubbard, L., & Lintz, A. (1996). *Constructing school suc-*

cess: The consequences of untracking low-achieving students. Cambridge: Cambridge University Press.

Mellor, N. A. (2001). *Orchids in the desert: An interpretive study of the role of the future in the lives of selected Mexican American students who live in the Central San Joaquin Valley, California.* Unpublished doctoral dissertation, University of San Francisco.

Merton, R. (1957). *Social theory and social structure.* New York: Free Press.

Murray, C. (2007a, January 16). Intelligence in the classroom. *Wall Street Journal.* Retrieved October 3, 2007, from http://www.opinionjournal.com/extra/?id=110009531/

Murray, C. (2007b, January 17). What's wrong with vocational school? *Wall Street Journal.* Retrieved October 3, 2007, from http://www.opinionjournal.com/extra/?id=110009535/

Murray, C. (2007c, January 18). Aztecs vs. Greeks. *Wall Street Journal.* Retrieved October 3, 2007, from http://www.opinionjournal.com/extra/?id=110009541/

Nansel, T., Overpeck, M., Pilla, R., Ruan, W., Simons-Morton, B., & Scheidt, P. (2001). Bullying behaviors among U.S. youth: Prevalence and association with psychosocial adjustment. *Journal of the American Medical Association, 285*(16), 2094–2100.

Ogbu, J. U. (2003). *Black American students in an affluent suburb: A study of academic disengagement.* Nahwah, NJ: Lawrence Erlbaum.

Ogbu, J. U. (2004). Collective identity and the burden of "acting white" in Black history, community, and education. *The Urban Review, 36*(1), 1–35.

Ogbu, J. U., & Simons, D. H. (1998). Voluntary and involuntary minorities: A cultural-ecological theory of school performance with some implications for education. *Anthropology & Education Quarterly, 29*(2), 155–188.

Pascarella, E. T., & Terenzini, P. T. (1991). *How college affects students: Findings and insights from twenty years of research.* San Francisco: Jossey-Bass.

Perlstein, D. (2004, Spring). Politics and historical imagination. In Teaching *Brown*: Reflections on pedagogical challenges and opportunities [special issue]. *History of Education Quarterly, 44.* Retrieved May 17, 2007, from http://www.trincoll.edu/depts/educ/brown/perlstein.htm

Perry, T., Steele, C., & Hilliard A., III. (2003). *Young, gifted, and Black: Promoting high achievement among African-American students.* Boston: Beacon Press.

Peters, R. S. (1967). *Ethics and education.* Glenview: IL: Scott, Foresman.

Petersen, W. (1966, January 9). Success story, Japanese-American style. *New York Times Magazine,* pp. 20–43.

Peterson, J. S., & Ray, K. E. (2006). Bullying and the gifted: Victims, perpetrators, prevalence, and effects. *Gifted Child Quarterly, 50*(2), 148–168.

Policy Analysis for California Education (PACE). (2004, April). *Improving the transition from high school to postsecondary education* (Working Paper Series No. 04-01). Berkeley, CA: Author.

Pollock, M. (2004). *Colormute: Race talk dilemmas in an American school.* Princeton: Princeton University Press.

Pollock, M. (2005). Keeping on keeping on: OCR and complaints of racial discrimination 50 years after *Brown. Teachers College Record, 107*(9), 2106–2140.

Prince, M., & Hoyt, B. (2002, November). Helping students make the transition from novice to expert problem-solvers. Paper presented at the 32nd ASEE/IEEE Frontiers in Education Conference, Boston.

Reid, S. (2007, April 11). Snoop Dogg says rappers and Imus are "two separate things." *MTV News*. Retrieved May 6, 2007, from http://www.mtv.com/news/articles/1556803/20070410/id_0.jhtml

Rose, M. (1989). *Lives on the boundary: A moving account of the struggles and achievements of America's educational underclass*. New York: Free Press.

Rugg, H. (1924). The curriculum for gifted children. In G. M. Whipple (Ed.), *Twenty-third yearbook of the National Society for the Study of Education: Part 1. The education of gifted children* (pp. 91–121). Bloomington, IL: Public School Publishing.

Sackett, P., Mardison, C. M., & Cullen, M. J. (2004). On interpreting stereotype threat as accounting for African American–White differences on cognitive tests. *American Psychologist, 59*(1), 7–13.

Santoro, N. (2005, October 24). When does race matter?: Teachers engaging in "race talk." [Review of the book *Colormute: Race talk dilemmas in an American school*]. *Australian Review of Public Affairs*. Retrieved October 3, 2007, from http://www.australianreview.net/digest/2005/10/santoro.html

Schemo, D. J. (2006, August 9). On education; It takes more than schools to close the achievement gap. *New York Times*. Retrieved May 17, 2007 from http://select.nytimes.com/search/restricted/article?res= F60A17FE345B0C7A8CDDA10894 DE404482

Sears, P. S. (1979). The Terman genetic studies of genius, 1922–1972. In A. H. Passow (Ed.), *Seventy-eighth yearbook of the National Society for the Study of Education: Part 1. The gifted and the talented: Their education and development* (pp. 75–96). Chicago: University of Chicago Press.

Simon, H. A., & Chase, W. G. (1973). Skill in chess. *American Scientist, 61*, 394–403.

Simonton, D. K. (2003). When does giftedness become genius? And when not? In N. Colangelo & G. A. Davis (Eds.), *Handbook of gifted education* (3rd ed., pp. 358–370). Boston: Allyn & Bacon.

Skocpol, T. (1999, May). Civic groups fostered citizenship and political engagement. *Public Affairs Report, 40*(3). Retrieved May 17, 2007, from http://www.igs.berkeley.edu/publications/par/2/skocpol.html

Sosniak, L. A. (1985). A long-term commitment to learning. In B. S. Bloom (Ed.), *Developing talent in young people* (pp. 477–506). New York: Ballantine.

Sosniak, L. A. (1987). The nature of change in successful learning. *Teachers College Record, 88*(4), 519–535.

Sosniak, L. A. (1995). Inviting adolescents into academic communities: An alternative perspective on systemic reform. *Theory Into Practice, 34*(1), 35–42.

Steele, C. M. (1998). Stereotype threat and the intellectual test performance of African Americans. *Journal of Personality & Social Psychology, 69*, 797–811.

Steele, C. M., & Aronson, J. (1995). Stereotype threat and the test performance of academically successful African Americans. In C. Jenks & M. Phillips (Eds.),

The Black-White test score gap (pp. 401–427). Washington, DC: Brookings Institution.

Subotnik, R., Kassan, L., Summers, E., & Wasser, A. (1993). *Genius revisited: High IQ children grown up*. Norwood, NJ: Ablex.

Success story of one minority group in the U.S. (1966, December 26). *U.S. News & World Report*, 158–163.

Tannenbaum, A. J. (1958). History of interest in the gifted. In N. B. Henry (Ed.), *Fifty-seventh yearbook of the National Society for the Study of Education: Part 2. Education for the gifted* (pp. 21–38). Chicago: University of Chicago Press.

Teachers who ROCK. (2006, December). *California Educator*. Burlingame, CA: California Teachers Association.

Terman, L. M. (1925). *Genetic studies of genius: Vol. 1. Mental and physical traits of a thousand gifted children*. Stanford, CA: Stanford University Press.

Thernstrom, M. (2005, February 13). The new arranged marriage. *New York Times Magazine*, pp. 34–41, 72–78.

Tusting, K. (2005). Language and power in communities of practice. In D. Barton & K. Tusting (Eds.), *Beyond communities of practice: Language power and social context* (pp. 39–42). New York: Cambridge University Press.

U.S. Department of Education. (1993). *National excellence: A case for developing America's talent*. Washington, DC: Author.

U.S. Department of Education. (2003a, June). *The condition of education 2003*. Washington, D.C.: Author.

U.S. Department of Education. (2003b, June). *Digest of education statistics 2002*. Washington, D.C.: Author.

Valenzuela, A. (1999). *Subtractive schooling: U.S.-Mexican youth and the policy of caring*. Albany: State University of New York Press.

Webb, E. T., Campbell, D. T., Schwartz, R. D., Sechrest, L., & Grove, J. B. (1981). *Nonreactive measures in the social sciences* (2nd ed.). Boston: Houghton Mifflin.

Weinstein, R. S. (2002). *Reaching higher: The power of expectations in schooling*. Cambridge, MA: Harvard University Press.

Wenger, E., McDermott, R., & Snyder, W. M. (2002). *Cultivating communities of practice*. Boston: Harvard Business School Press.

Westheimer, J., & Kahne, J. (2004). What kind of a citizen? The politics of educating for democracy. *American Educational Journal*, 41(2), 237–269.

Whitehead, A. N. (1929). *The aims of education*. New York: Macmillan.

Wiseman, R. (2007, February 25). How to fight the new bullies. *Parade.com*. Retrieved October 3, 2007, from http://www.parade.com/articles/editions/2007/edition_02-25-2007/cyberbullying

Worrell, F. C. (2003). Why are there so few African Americans in gifted education programs? In C. C. Yeakey & R. D. Henderson (Eds.), *Surmounting all odds: Education, opportunity, and society in the new millennium* (Vol. 2). Greenwich: Information Age Publishing.

Worrell, F. C., Szarko, J. E., & Gabelko, N. H. (2001). Multi-year persistence of nontraditional students in an academic talent development program. *Journal of Secondary Gifted Education*, 12(2), 80–89.

Wu, F. H. (2002). *Yellow: Race in America beyond Black and White.* New York: Basic Books.

Zeidner, M., & Schleyer, E. J. (1999). The big-fish-little-pond effect for academic self-concept, test anxiety, and school grades in gifted children. *Contemporary Educational Psychology, 24,* 305–329.

Zettel, J. (1979). State provisions for educating the gifted and talented. In A. H. Passow (Ed.), *Seventy-eighth yearbook of the National Society for the Study of Education: Part 1. The gifted and the talented: Their education and development* (pp. 63–74). Chicago: University of Chicago Press.

Index

About the Authors

LAUREN A. SOSNIAK (deceased), a familiar name in talent development research, was a professor of education at San José State University in California. For over a decade, she wrote about the Academic Talent Development Program at the University of California at Berkeley, where she was a visiting professor.

NINA HERSCH GABELKO has been director of the Academic Talent Development Program at the University of California at Berkeley for over 20 years, and has been a lecturer in Berkeley's Graduate School of Education since 1985.